THE

BOOK

OF

ESPORTS

THE OFFICIAL HISTORY

OF ESPORTS™

BY

WILLIAM COLLIS

Rosetta
Books®

First edition published 2020 by RosettaBooks

Jacket and interior design by Christian Fuenfhausen

ISBN-13 (print): 978-1-9481-2257-3
ISBN-13 (ebook): 978-1-9481-2258-0

Library of Congress Cataloging-in-Publication Data
Names: Collis, William, author.
Title: The book of esports : the official history of esports / by William
Collis.
Description: First edition. | New York : RosettaBooks, 2020. | Includes
bibliographical references. |
Identifiers: LCCN 2020014979 (print) | LCCN 2020014980 (ebook) | ISBN
9781948122573 (hardcover) | ISBN 9781948122580 (ebook)
Subjects: LCSH: Esports (Contests)--History.
Classification: LCC GV1469.34.E86 C65 2020 (print) | LCC GV1469.34.E86
(ebook) | DDC 794.8--dc23

www.RosettaBooks.com
Printed in Canada

I dedicate this book to all my family:
past, present, and future.

"Some are born great, some achieve greatness, and some have greatness thrust upon them."

—William Shakespeare, *Twelfth Night*, Act 5, Scene 1

CONTENTS

Part III: A New Challenger Appears!

FOREWORD

BY PAUL DAWALIBI

I knew the day I met William that he would be the person to write the definitive book on esports. I've always called him "The Professor" because William is the exact type of person you would want to teach you history or tell you a story. He has a talent for making words come alive, and communicating even the most abstract concepts in ways that are easy to understand. And most of all, he knows esports, having raised millions in venture capital to grow two successful businesses in the space.

Today, William and I host the (now world-famous) podcast The Business of Esports. And I can attest, after thousands of hours together, that William's love of esports is no act. He really is as nerdy as he seems, and he really does know this industry better than anyone alive today.

This book is the perfect foundation for anyone interested in gaming as a hobby, anyone whose industry might be affected by gaming, and anyone who will need to market to gamers and understand their world. It's even perfect for parents trying to understand what exactly it is their son or daughter is doing all day. William has laid out the future of digital competition, and how it reshapes lives and businesses today.

Carl Sagan once famously said, "You have to know the past to understand the present." Never has this been more true than with esports. By explaining gaming's history, William helps us appreciate how humanity itself is changing. And how esports is catalyzing this change.

Isn't it time you learned what esports are all about?

— **Paul "The Esports Profit" Dawalibi**

PROLOGUE:
PRESS START

We strive for the exceptional.

That, in its essence, is our nature as humans. We aren't interested in the mundane, the typical, or the amateur. We don't celebrate that which is familiar or frequent. Instead, we crave the unlimited and the extraordinary. Those rare glimpses of raw skill that make us question the boundaries of what it means to be human.

For all of known history, this drive has propelled humanity onward. To art and invention. To creation and conflict. And perhaps most of all, to sport.

Technology has always played its part in our games and competitions. Arenas have evolved from muddied pitches to storied stadia. Refereeing has transformed from gentlemen's honor to instant replays. Even the act of watching sports has been radically transformed by digital broadcasts.

But always one thing was constant: the human.

For we still competed in reality.

Sports remained bound by the fundamental coefficients of physics and the mortal laws of life and death. Science acted like a blunt instrument: artificially extending athletic careers with tendon-transplant surgeries, or improving equipment designs to cushion concussive blows. But by and large, despite the incredible innovation characterizing our twenty-first century, sports remained surprisingly anachronistic. Still tamed by reality.

Until now. Until esports.

Make no mistake: we are entering a new world, brave and bold. As laptops and smartphones have digitized our daily lives, human competition now leaps this electronic divide.

You hold in your hands the testament of a new generation of human competition. *The Book of Esports* is at once an overview of where we are, a celebration of how far we've come, and a prophecy for how far we will go as human competition radically evolves.

Everything is about to change.

Esports, or competitive video games, are not single-player experiences with memorizable level layouts. Instead, picture intricately choreographed teamwork, pixel-perfect commands, and brilliantly innovative strategies, all taking place in gloriously simulated environments, where the impossible is matter-of-fact and the spectacular is assured.

And just like there are dozens of genres of sport, ranging from mainstream (football) to niche (volleyball) to obscure (curling), there are similarly many genres of esports.

THE BIG FIVE

While there are dozens of types of esports, the "big five" genres dominate the industry today: *first-person shooters, battle royales, MOBAs, collectible card games,* and *fighters*. We'll cover these genres, and more, in detail throughout the book. But right now, here's a quick summary of each to get you up to speed:

First-person shooters (FPSs) are gun-based titles emphasizing accuracy and reflexes. They are modernized versions of classics like *Doom* and

Wolfenstein, but far more difficult to play because of their fast-paced, 360-degree aiming and team tactics.

Battle royales are similar to FPSs, but feature chaotic everyone-for-themselves combat, played from either a first- or third-person perspective, across a large-scale, but constantly shrinking, battle arena. One of the most popular games in the world.—*Fortnite*—exemplifies this genre.

Multiplayer online battle arenas (MOBAs) involve teams of five players, each controlling a single character from a 3D isometric view and carefully sequencing their abilities to destroy opposing forces and overwhelm the opposing team's fortified base.

Collectible card games are purely strategic titles, where a sequence of virtual objects (usually cards) are played to a digital board. Each object has different powers and associated costs, requiring careful planning and sequencing to maximize their efficacy.

Fighting games are modernized versions of the original arcade hit *Street Fighter*. They feature two players dueling with martial arts on a 2D or 3D plane. Of all genres of esports, fighters have changed the least since the early days of gaming.

All these games roll up into a $27 billion industry, backed by billion-dollar investments from Amazon, Facebook, Tencent, and more.[1] Picture ESPN-style broadcasts, full-ride academic scholarships, and multimillion-dollar prizing. Picture seven-figure endorsements with the likes of Louis Vuitton and BMW. Picture hundreds of millions of fans, most under thirty, clamoring for digital victory.

But esports are so much more than big business. For the first time ever, human competition is shedding its most ancient burden: the body. With esports, we no longer need to care about the frailty of flesh, or the random rewards of genetics. Too short to play basketball, or too old to play football? Don't worry.

In esports, the athlete is the brain. Anyone who can use a keyboard, mouse, or controller can compete.

That is why you must read this book. And why you must care about esports.

Not because it is one of the fastest-growing entertainment industries of all time. Not because more people watch esports than the NBA or MLB.[2] Not because its celebrities command followings so large they sell out global product lines with a single tweet. Not because our children play these games and idolize these gamers. Not even because of the most fundamental truth: esports are really fun.

No. You need to read this book because esports is the beginning of the democratization of all sport, as a whole. Because the way humans compete is being forever altered by the fairness of digital avatars and rendered worlds. Today hand-eye coordination and digital dexterity still matter, but soon even these slim barriers will cease. Esports hints at an egalitarian future, where superstar potential is determined by drive alone, and where the limits of the body are undone at last.

Welcome to the future. Welcome to *The Book of Esports*.

ESPORTS 101

This book assumes at least a casual familiarity with video games. But don't worry if you feel a bit lost or overwhelmed while reading. The back of the book provides an informative **APPENDIX** that neatly summarizes the basics of modern gaming and esports in a few short pages. Feel free to turn to this section now if you'd like a little extra background. This **APPENDIX** is not required by any means, but it can prove a helpful foundation for a neophyte.

PART I

A BRIEF HISTORY OF 1-UPS

CHAPTER ONE

THE BITS AT THE BEGINNING

The Staples Center, Los Angeles, 2013.

More than fifteen thousand fans fill the coliseum seating, chanting with a passion that shakes the building's foundations. Strobe lights and neon signs flash as the athletes take center stage. Blake Griffin and Jordan Hill played here just last week, but there will be no basketball tonight.

Instead, ten computers claim center court, blaring a multitude of iridescent insignia. Tonight, instead of seven-foot-tall titans, spectacle-wearing youths stride center stage. And the crowd explodes.

In 2013, the *League of Legends* Finals at the Staples Center ushered in the first watershed moment of modern esports. For the first time ever, what had been a secret battlefield taking place across far-flung digital servers was given a tangible manifestation in the Western world. There had been major esports tournaments before, but this spectacle in particular became lodged into the public consciousness. The mainstream media took notice of what thirty-two million online viewers already knew:

The rise of esports had begun.

Just a year later, Amazon would create the industry's first billion-dollar company, buying Twitch—the broadcaster, or streaming platform, of choice in esports—for almost a billion dollars. A little more than a year after that, the gold rush of esports would start with Shaquille O'Neal, Jennifer Lopez, and countless other celebrities investing in pro teams. And a year after that, traditional sports would leap in full steam ahead, with the NBA announcing an esports league for digital basketball, with six-figure salaries and nearly every franchised team creating a shadow roster of electronic athletes.

And this is just the tip of the iceberg. To truly understand the rise of esports, we need to appreciate the roots of gaming culture itself. We need to understand how competitive video games, even very good ones, have nearly always existed. We need to analyze the emerging digital ecosystems that allowed esports to evolve. And we need to trace the similarities between the gaming trends of yesteryear—like online guilds—into the development of modern gaming organizations. Because only by appreciating the past can we understand that esports *did not* come out of nowhere. Rather, esports are part of a steady trend of digital transformation in human play.

So let's begin at the beginning. With a ball.

Tracing the evolution of esports back, we find an unexpected origin story. Esports didn't begin in some dark basement with adolescent children yelling at a blue-lit screen. Nor did it catalyze with clever developers crafting a marketing plan to make their latest blockbuster game even more addictive.

Esports started in a bar in 1947, with a twist on the classic pinball machine.[1] Coin-operated games had been around since early slot machines, dating back as far as 1894 (and perhaps even earlier). Mechanical pinball itself was over a decade old at this point. So what made this particular 1947 machine so special as it debuted in pubs across the United Kingdom? Flippers!

Previous iterations of pinball units were simple. You launched a metal ball, just as we do today, into the main section of the cabinet and watched it bounce off pins and bumpers until, eventually, it would fall into one of a dozen point-yielding pockets.

And that was it. Pinball never progressed past this level of elementary play. Sure, some versions encouraged players to bump and tilt the machine, but many people, including the US government, were more inclined to relate the mechanics of pinball to gambling at a casino.[2]

So, why did the addition of a few plastic wedges vault pinball into a keystone of English pubs? Because it introduced the idea of *control*.

Humans love games of chance. There is something fun and addictive—in the worst kind of way, perhaps—in putting it all on black at the roulette wheel. But there is a reason why there isn't a world championship for roulette.

Games that incorporate player control introduce the possibility of *skill*. By being able to affect the outcome of a pinball machine directly, suddenly bar patrons weren't just *watching* pinball, they were *playing* it. And this simple requirement— *skill*—is the first driving force in our narrative of esports.

In total, there are four factors (which we'll call **SCAR** factors) that propelled the rise of competitive gaming:

Skill – The talent and time required to master a game.

Community – The support a game receives from its creators and fans.

Accessibility – The barriers to purchase and learn a game.

Reward – The benefits for getting good at a game.

We'll address each SCAR factor in greater detail as we move through the book. But for now, we're going to stick with pinball.

With the introduction of flippers, pinball became a game of skill. And as London pub regulars quickly discovered, it was possible to get good at pinball. It became a badge of honor to hold a high score at your favorite bar. The arbitrary numbers on the pinball machine began to take on meaning, and a life of their own, as something to be revered.

Consider The Who's 1969 rock opera *Tommy*, the moving story of a boy with a disability transformed into a hero who becomes "part of the machine." The main song, "Pinball Wizard," became a cultural touchpoint for the pinball mania sweeping the world. This story arguably marks the dawn of esports, because gaming had found its first celebrity, if a fictional one.

We begin with pinball to highlight that humanity—and what we appreciate and value—has not changed. Even in the 1960s, a desire to revere gaming skill could capture the hearts of the world. "Pinball Wizard" endures so well today because it isn't really about the game. It's about the person playing it.

Google "What was the first video game ever?" and *Pong* shows at the top of the list. And in many ways, *Pong* is the direct evolution of pinball into the digital realm. It's a game about bouncing a ball using simulated physics, with a limited axis of player control. It was as good of an approximation of pinball as we were capable of creating digitally when it hit arcades in 1972.

But *Pong* was in fact *not* the first video game.

Technology experts had been tinkering with the idea of video-based games since the end of WWII. Massive binary computers, originally utilized for breaking complex German code, were repurposed for less critical but equally impressive uses. And so it was Josef Kates, an Austrian residing in Toronto postwar, who made history with the *actual* first-ever interactive computer game: *Bertie the Brain*. Revealed in 1950 at the Canadian National Exhibition, *Bertie* wasn't the prettiest piece of technology. But for the attendees of the exhibition, it didn't matter. People were awestruck to play the grade-school classic tic-tac-toe with an automated opponent who, if cranked to maximum difficulty, was impossible to defeat. And while many video game historians and experts knock *Bertie the Brain*'s legitimacy as a video game, it's undeniable that this thirteen-foot metal giant paved the way for the future of interactive media.[3]

More innovations followed quickly. In 1951, the custom-built Nimrod machine successfully played *Nim*, the classic line elimination game. Soon after, Cambridge University's EDSAC simulated tic-tac-toe on a real computer screen, advancing *Bertie*'s lightbulb design. Next, Brookhaven National Laboratory demonstrated *Tennis for Two* in 1958, introducing real-time gameplay with simulated ball movement.

However, none of these advancements were as important or as impressive as what was to come.

Spacewar!, introduced in 1962, was pivotal to gaming history. Not necessarily because of the game itself, but because of the technological advances that made *Spacewar!* possible. Up to that point, video games took up the same amount of space as a small toolshed. Not exactly something that could be wrapped and put under the Christmas tree. But in the early 1950s, transistors changed computing technology forever. The word might not sound impressive now, but transistors are one of the main reasons you or I own a personal computer today.

Computers work through myriad electronic switches. The

switches pass along binary information—basically a series of off and on electrical pulses—that computers read and respond to. Old-school computers used bulb-sized glass tubes with wiring inside of them, called vacuum tubes, to send these signals. And first-generation computers needed a lot of these to work— around 20,000 of them. To make matters worse, vacuum tubes were power inefficient and prone to error.

Not only were transistors a fraction of the price of vacuum tubes, they were also fast, the size of a fingernail, and extremely reliable. They made computers better in almost every way: they became smaller, quicker, and cheaper.

So in 1961, the Digital Equipment Corporation (DEC) shared PDP-1, one of the first computers to use transistors, with the brilliant minds at the Massachusetts Institute of Technology (MIT). And PDP-1 was so revolutionary, it afforded researcher Steve Russell something he'd never had before: free time.

Previously, computers were slow, and so constantly crunching numbers. But the PDP-1 could do its calculations so fast it simply wasn't needed all the time for important work. It sat idle.

Russell wondered what he might *do* with the most powerful computer in the world, when it wasn't *doing* anything at all. In 1962, inspired by science fiction, he led a team of fellow researchers and students to make *Spacewar!* This game was different not just because it was a work of coding genius, but because it wasn't trying to simulate previously existing games, like *Nim* or tic-tac-toe. It was its own digital creation, a simulation of interstellar dogfighting.

Spacewar! was an instant hit amongst researchers at MIT. And, because of the magic of transistors, it was a hit that spread.

Spacewar! soon found its way to dozens of computers around the country. Whether by sharing code or reverse engineering, *Spacewar!* became an awe-inspiring piece of pandemic computer lab technology. Video games had just taken their first step away from singular novelties towards world domination.

Now we come to the second SCAR factor that has contributed to the rise of esports: *accessibility.*

Spacewar! was arguably the first accessible video game. You could share it with anyone else who had a transistor computer. Steve Russell brought *Spacewar!* with him wherever he went, including to Stanford University in 1972, where the campus became so enraptured that its artificial intelligence lab held its own *Spacewar!* competition.

These Intergalactic Olympics featured three events: a five-player free-for-all, duos, and a one-versus-one bracket competition. The prize for taking down this inaugural event was a year-long subscription to *Rolling Stone* magazine.

It likely wouldn't have felt to the dozen or so graduate students gaming away the afternoon that they were making history, but they certainly were. These Intergalactic Olympics hinted that computer games were not simply for solitary play, but worthy of challenge. For the first time ever, a *community* (the third SCAR factor) formed around video games, albeit a narrow one. The Intergalactic Olympics wasn't about its meager prize, but the brotherhood of the battle.

So why does *Pong* come up when Googling "first video game"? Because *Pong* did an even better job than *Spacewar!* at being accessible. *Spacewar!* was insanely popular amongst privileged academics, but to become a true phenomenon, video games needed to reach mass distribution, which required low-cost production.

The Herculean task of taking *Spacewar!* to the general public fell to two devotees, Bill Pitts and Hugh Tuck. Their approach was direct: just put PDP computers into arcades. Of course, right away there was a problem. The cheapest PDP computer still cost over $20,000 in 1972 (about $125,000 today).

The pair hoped that despite the expensive price tag, the popularity of a *Spacewar!* machine would compensate. But to put it bluntly, the quarters just didn't add up. Finding themselves $65,000 in the hole and still unable to solve the pricing issue, Pitts and Tuck yielded production of a second prototype, and ultimately their dream of spreading the sci-fi legend.

If gaming was going to go mainstream, it was clear that someone had to figure out how to make games cheaper.

Enter Nolan Bushnell and Ted Dabney. This intrepid pair of entrepreneurs set out to create a prototype *Spacewar!* cabinet that didn't require a mortgage to acquire. The breakthrough came by refashioning general-purpose computer design to include only the components in a PDP-powered cabinet essential to play a homegrown version of *Spacewar!*, now being called *Computer Space*. The more affordable $1,000 unit seemed like the golden key to unlocking the popularity of video games.

Or was it?

"Lackluster" is probably the best way to describe the 1971 commercial release of *Computer Space*. At most, 1,500 units were sold. The arcade machine wasn't a total disaster, but it definitively underperformed the average pinball machine (which sold approximately 2,000 installs at that time).

What was holding *Computer Space* back? The answer is still accessibility. Just a different kind.

Computer Space may have been affordable, but that didn't mean it was playable. The game's control scheme was unintuitive and confusing, especially for the average user (who had never interacted with a computer before). This challenge was compounded by the fact that *Computer Space*'s manufacturer, Nutting Associates, hadn't done a good job of marketing the game, and a critical function of the game's marketing was supposed to be teaching players how to control it.

Rather than give up, Nolan and Ted set out to do better. Taking the $150,000 they had personally pocketed from *Computer Space* sales, they founded their own independent company. They called it Atari, a term from the popular East Asian board game Go that can also mean "lucky win" in Japanese.

The partners set out to develop a new game with intuitive controls to appeal to their neophyte audience. At first, they were interested in developing racers, believing driving to be more instinctive than navigating a spaceship. But after seeing an early demo of the Magnavox Odyssey, one of the first home video game consoles, inspiration struck. Nolan assigned his first Atari employee, Allan Alcorn, the task of developing an improved version of digital ping-pong as Atari's first game. And *Pong* was born.

Pong is often cited as the first video game because it was the first to be widely played. Atari sold nearly 8,000 arcade machines in its early years. But the most impressive success of *Pong* wasn't just unit sales, but the popularity of each individual machine.

Pong competed with the pinball craze, which was in full swing in the early 1970s. A successful pinball machine grossed about fifty dollars a week, but *Pong* cabinets were so popular they shattered this record, earning nearly $300. While pinball cabinets might host twenty players a night, *Pong* could boast upward of 120. Almost overnight, *Pong* became the most popular arcade game on the planet. Pinball arcades were finished. Gaming arcades were the future.

The community sparked with the Intergalactic Olympics was about to undergo rapid expansion. The ingredients for competitive gaming, even in the early 1970s, started to form. They had a long way to go, but the outlook was positive.

Even as early as the 1970s, three of the four SCAR factors—skill, community, and accessibility—that drive modern esports were coming into being. Our journey had begun.

CHAPTER TWO:

SAVING THE PRINCESS

A fundamental reality of modern society is that we prefer things at home. From Netflix to Amazon, today's most valuable companies are largely built around the convenience of delivering things you love to your doorstep.

In the 1970s, people were no different. *Pong* was popular, but it would be *more* popular if you could play it at home. And so the accessibility of games was about to take another quantum leap forward.

Almost as soon as people realized the magic of gaming, companies tried to design cost-effective ways to bring it into living rooms everywhere. The need was obvious. What could be better than your very own personal arcade machine, played from the comfort of your couch?

In 1972 the Magnavox Odyssey became the first true home console. The Odyssey differentiated itself from earlier competitors in a critical way: it hooked into a standard TV set (hence Magnavox in the console's name). Suddenly, arcades seemed obsolete. Now you could wake up on a lazy Sunday and enjoy the thrill of a multi-bit adventure at home.

But TV connectivity didn't just bring consoles into the living room; critically, this feature also reduced their price. Now there was no longer a need to also pay for an unwieldy vector display alongside the gaming unit itself. You could leverage the TV set you already owned to get a better visual experience at a lower price.

The Magnavox Odyssey debuted at the incredible price point of $99.99 (or $49.99, if purchased with a Magnavox television). Unsurprisingly, the home console market exploded. Odyssey sales reached up to 100,000 units in their first year, and Atari didn't take the competition lying down. In 1975, they entered the home market, selling nearly 150,000 units of their home *Pong* system in a single holiday season. By 1977, sales of Atari's newest console grew to 400,000 units.

Naturally, the rapid expansion of home consoles drew wide corporate interest and investment. Over the next decade, literally dozens of consoles launched with hundreds of novel games. From *Breakout* by Steve Wozniak and Steve Jobs to *Space Invaders* (which itself became a milestone for spectator-driven play), industry growth skyrocketed.[1]

But these good times belied danger. Throughout the 1970s, graphics got better and hardware cheaper, but fundamentally home gaming remained in its infancy. In the 1970s, novelty mattered more than quality, and the thrill of playing on a television set outweighed what exactly you were playing.

Put simply, most games dating from the 1970s lacked one particular SCAR factor: skill. Titles were relatively basic, and although they might take some talent to play, they offered only temporarily rewarding experiences. Once the wonder of controlling pixels on a TV screen wore off, you were left with a title like *Dragster*, played by essentially mashing a single button.

Early gaming had entered a bubble. And that bubble was about to pop.

By 1982, numerous home console manufacturers had emerged. Atari, Magnavox, Coleco, Mattel Electronics, and more all produced their own multitude of consoles, each incompatible, and all with a dizzying array of both in-house and third-party-developed games, often with disastrous quality control.[2]

A fragmented and confused consumer base posed a unique risk, compounded by the fact that console manufacturers had to produce in advance of demand, guessing at the size of each sales cycle. And given the rapid growth of the industry, console manufacturers were in full-on build mode. The sky seemed the limit.

The next two years were a gaming apocalypse. In under three years, the annual revenue of the video game industry declined 60 percent, from a peak of nearly $25 billion in 1982 to a nadir of $10 billion by 1985. The once-hot home entertainment industry lay on its deathbed, part of a larger decline in the entire gaming market.

E.T. PHONE HOME?

One of the most infamously terrible titles of 1982 was the video game adaptation of *E.T. The Extra-Terrestrial* by Atari. Although originally conceptualized as an ambitious and innovative project, a delay in securing the rights resulted in less than two months of development time. The game had been planned as a huge success, but its quality was so terrible that millions of unsold cartridges were eventually buried in the New Mexico desert. Today, *E.T.* is often remembered as one of the worst-ever games produced.

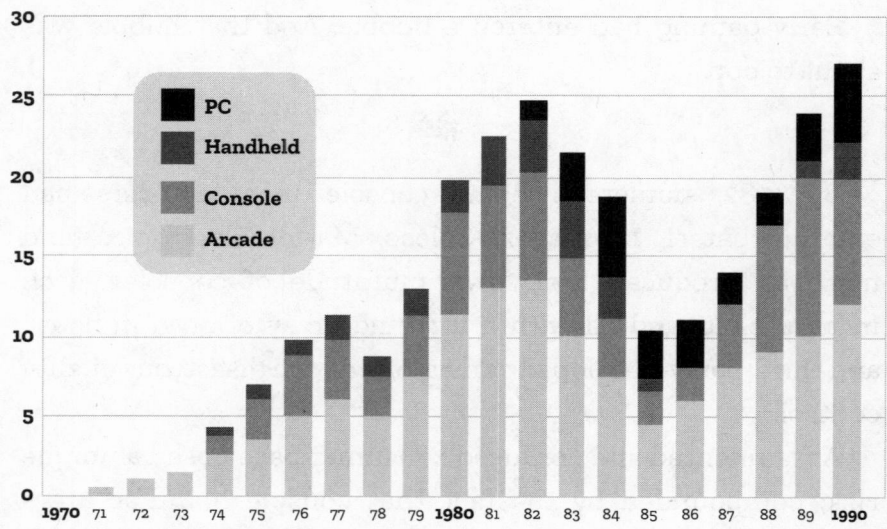

The massive collapse of the video game industry across just three years, between 1982 and 1985.

To be sure, there were many problems facing consoles: The emerging home computer industry. Knock-offs and unauthorized vendors. Even the declining popularity of arcades (caused, ironically, by consoles).

But the biggest problem was simple: The games sucked. Like in the early days of pinball machines, someone needed to invent the flippers.

It's an incredible coincidence that the saving grace of the console industry was none other than the "hand of fate" itself—a loose translation of the name of the Japanese brand Nintendo.

Originally founded in 1889, Nintendo seemed the *least* likely candidate to reshape the video game industry. For nearly seventy years before this, Nintendo had made a name for itself producing playing cards. But the company had little to do with electronics.

"The 1970s was an era of huge growth in Japan," explains the preeminent Japanese academic Tomo Noda, founder of Shizenkan University in Tokyo. "There was a sense of limitless challenge and continuous innovation, in which many companies completely reinvented themselves postwar for the global markets. Nintendo was part of this emerging breed of Japanese company. All of Japan was rebuilding. Why not Nintendo, too? The company imagined itself not as a playing card company, but as a *game* company. And in the early 80s, the hottest trend in gaming was consoles. Even better, Japan was a hotbed for the electronics industry, leading to earlier and lower-cost innovation access for domestic producers. The marriage between Nintendo and video games must have seemed crazy, but it was also perfect."

In 1981, Nintendo jumped into the gaming market as a third-party developer, launching two games just before the market crash. One title, in particular, is legendary: *Donkey Kong*. Even in modern times, the high-score record on an original *Donkey Kong* arcade cabinet remains controversially contested, with its spectacular rivalries and cheating accusations spanning decades (and featured in popular documentaries such as *The King of Kong*.)

Although a sophomoric effort, *Donkey Kong* proved Nintendo had a natural gift for designing games. *Donkey Kong* required

THE MYTHICAL JAPANESE COIN CRISIS

In 1980, *Space Invaders* was released worldwide. And while the game was a blockbuster nearly everywhere, it was especially popular in Japan. It was so popular, in fact, that some newspapers began to report the game was causing a shortage of 100-yen coins. While this claim is farfetched, some economists still find a correlation between the 1980s arcade craze and a drastic increase in newly minted yen coins. Whether fact or fiction, this story illustrates the enormous popularity of arcades in their heyday.

skill. Not a lot, but by the standards of the 1980s more than enough.

But Nintendo's timing could not have been worse. *Donkey Kong*'s success convinced the company to jump full steam ahead into the home console market.

Right as the console bubble burst.

Nintendo would have been wiped out, except for one unique advantage. The company didn't launch their first at-home console, the Famicom (short for family computer) globally. They launched it in Japan.

Japan was uniquely positioned in 1983. It boasted both a massive domestic market (the third-largest in the world) and a rapidly accelerating wage rate that permitted luxury spending. Nintendo didn't *need* the rest of the world to buy its products. Much as Japanese car companies built global dominance on the back of domestic demand, Nintendo did the same for video games.

The Famicom launched to explosive popularity in Japan, selling millions of consoles within its first two years. Buoyed by this success, Nintendo did the unthinkable. They prepared to launch the unit in America (rebranded as the Nintendo Entertainment System, or NES), at the very nadir of gaming's international collapse. How did Nintendo pull off this miracle, even as the gaming market burned down around them?

True to the console's new name, Nintendo created an entertainment system by also redesigning the Famicom for an international market. In particular, Nintendo made two critical improvements.

First, they designed "toy-like" game cartridges that docked into the console. While cartridges had been around since the inception of home consoles, they were often little more than switches—not true memory or game storage units. Nintendo didn't invent the idea of selling games independently from consoles, but they were the first to perfect this practice—making swapping games painless and even fun.

Second, Nintendo instituted strict quality control across its gaming ecosystem. Noticing the proliferation of low-grade third-party titles, Nintendo required that every game launching on the NES obtain a Nintendo Seal of Quality. Nintendo also highly regulated the process of third-party development, ensuring that consumers could trust every game they bought. In turn, the Nintendo Seal of Quality also made it difficult for unlicensed third parties and knock-offs to clone cartridges.

With these two strategic decisions, the NES both made life better for consumers and created a significant quality advantage against competitors. As a result, Nintendo could now effectively employ a razor-and-blades business model.

In the razor-and-blades model, consumers make a big one-time purchase—razors, or in this case the console—at a low cost. But the manufacturer makes up the difference with future sales—blade replacements, or in this case games. By charging a lower upfront price, the manufacturer sacrifices short-term revenue for improved accessibility, resulting in larger market share and greater long-term profits.

The *razor-and-blades* model is critical to understanding the rise of esports. It is one of just four monetization models by which the game companies make money. Just as the four SCAR factors determine the rise of esports as a whole, the four **BAMS models** chart the success of companies within the industry. The BAMS models are:

Blades – The razor-and-blades revenue model we have just seen, in which subsidized platforms (consoles) capture market share to lock in long-term sales (game cartridges).

Advertising and assets – A media revenue model in which games are monetized like traditional sports through advertising and the sale of broadcast rights.

Microtransactions – An evolution of the razor-and-blades revenue model, in which the games themselves become sales platforms, generating revenue by selling incremental enhancements to their gameplay. Microtransactions were heavily popularized by the mobile industry, and often involve giving away the game as a free download (a so-called "freemium" game).

Subscriptions – A "magazine-style" revenue model, in which customers subscribe to a game by paying recurring fees, often charged annually and in advance, in return for regular access to evolving content.

Because Nintendo perfected the blades revenue model, they gained a significant price and quality advantage against the competition. In turn, this improved the accessibility of gaming, making it cheaper to buy consoles and easier to discover fun games. But these improvements weren't Nintendo's only contribution to the gaming industry's revival. The decision to institute a Seal of Quality program also had a critical, secondary effect: it led to better games!

In arcades, the profitability of games was driven by coins per hour. More quarters, more money. This meant that good (as in high-grossing) games had simple and fast gameplay loops, resulting in quick deaths, high cycle times, and more revenue.

Up until the launch of the NES, most home console experiences were essentially ports of arcade titles. In other words, quick, disposable experiences, not the sorts of games that could stand up to repeated, at-home play. *Pong* and *Space Invaders* just don't work when you have hours to devote yourself to the experience. When playing at home, consumers wanted games they could sink their teeth into and improve with. In short, they wanted games that required skill.

The Nintendo Seal of Quality forced manufacturers—both Nintendo and their licensed third parties—to make games that were better than disposable arcade ports, with deeper, longer, and more complicated experiences. Games weren't sports yet, but they were maturing as entertainment.

It's no wonder then that the launch of the NES in America was nothing short of a miracle. While most gaming companies were closing down, the NES sold tens of thousands of units within its first few weeks in market. And within a few years, the NES had sold tens of millions *just* in the US, plus a slew of successful international releases. The NES singlehandedly resurrected the market for video games, while turning Nintendo into the global entertainment juggernaut it remains today.

In many ways, modern gaming dawned with Nintendo. For the first time, iconic characters were born: Zelda, Mario, and more. We know these heroes and their stories today because they were more than a disposable experience. They were enduring entertainment brands.

With Nintendo's success came a rich cycle of mimicry, innovation, and betrayal. Other companies, like Sega and Sony, piled into the market. The so-called "console wars" would define the next two decades of gaming, with consistent innovations in hardware power, game design, and (particularly in the case of Sega) marketing.

For our purposes, the console wars are largely meaningless because they focused on incremental improvements, not radical shifts. The jumps from 16-bit to 32-bit to 64-bit graphics, for example, seemed incredible in their time, but have

NINTENDON'T

Nintendo's biggest rival entered the console market in 1989, when Sega launched the Genesis (also called the Mega Drive in some international markets). Part of Sega's phenomenal success in challenging Nintendo's dominance was driven by its slogan: "Genesis does what Nintendon't." The branding worked, positioning Genesis as the more sophisticated and powerful platform geared toward older gamers. While it's arguable if these marketing claims were true, they kicked off the first conflict in a series of console wars, which continue to this day (although with different participants).

little historical value beyond the glaringly obvious insight that "more is better."

The course of the console gaming industry was set with the NES. So for the next two decades, graphics got flashier, games grew longer, mechanics balanced better, but not much fundamentally changed.

Except at the same time Nintendo fever was sweeping America, an unlikely innovation at the European Organization for Nuclear Research (CERN) was creating the next frontier in gaming. No one saw this technological shift as connected at the time. But nonetheless, a digital revolution was coming. . .

CHAPTER THREE

GUILDS AND GLORY

In 1989, Tim Berners-Lee invented the worldwide web while seeking a faster way to share academic data. From his lab at CERN, the innovation quickly spread to completely transform the modern world.

For most Western consumers, the internet entered our homes with America Online (AOL) in the early 1990s. AOL's chirpy dial-up noises and infamous e-mail tagline ("You've got mail!") became the gateway to digital connectivity. AOL grew so popular that at one point, 50 percent of all CDs produced featured the AOL logo.[1]

But AOL was founded in 1985. And Berners-Lee's breakthrough occurred in 1989. So what was AOL doing for four years, before the web existed? The answer is video games.

So far, we've discussed in detail two of the four SCAR factors required for the rise of esports: skill and accessibility. Now we'll take a closer look at a third, community, which is critical because it's the basis for all competition. And it was community that AOL set out to bring to gamers in 1985.

Then known as Quantum Computer Services, early AOL built a business hosting multiplayer games for the Commodore 64 and other first-generation consoles. The service wasn't good, but it was the best to be had in the 1980s. But because games were little more than disposable experiences, connecting gamers for competitive play didn't prove an industry-changing innovation. PlayNET knew how to make computers talk to one another, but gaming wasn't the best use for this technology. A quick business pivot later, AOL took their technology to home computers and a giant of early internet connectivity was born.

But AOL isn't important just because its gaming roots sparked our modern online world. AOL is also critical because its technology became the gateway for an entirely new genre of game: massive multiplayer online games, or MMOs.

In 1986, AOL's Quantum Link service partnered with Lucasfilms to produce *Habitat*, arguably the first-ever iteration of an online role-playing game. While the title may not have gone down in history as a classic, even in 1986 there was a clear desire to cross the digital divide and inhabit the incredible world of games with others.

GETTING MUDDY

MUDs, or multiuser dungeons, were another important precursor to modern MMOs. Originating in 1975 with *Colossal Cave Adventure*, developed by Will Crowther, they were essentially text-based adventure games, modeling Dungeons and Dragons, with a critical differentiating factor: They allowed players to talk to, and in many cases interact with, other users. They were essentially a chat room combined with a textual role-playing game, and they dominated university computer labs in the 1970s. "You haven't lived until you've died in MUD," ran the popular *MUD1* slogan, one of the leading titles in this micro-genre. Although blurring with campus life and natural user proximity (MUDs ran on local area networks), MUDs were still arguably the first instance of gamers making friends—and even falling in love—through digital worlds. The beginnings of a true gaming community.

The innovations laid out by *Habitat* and similar titles, from *Maze War* to MUDs, were too ambitious for their time. So the potential of online gaming worlds would lie dormant for almost a decade, until 1996 when *Meridian 59* debuted, quickly followed by the more popular *Ultima Online*, *EverQuest*, and *Asheron's Call*. These three games are typically referred to as the founding Trinity of MMOs.

These titles all took advantage of the rise of home internet to deliver rich, engrossing role-playing experiences, shared with others in interactive digital worlds. In particular, *EverQuest* emerged as the leader of the pack and by 2002 its estimated virtual GDP was as large as the country of Bulgaria.[2] In *EverQuest*, you could become a necromancer or a wizard, adventure to exotic lands, seize legendary treasures, and level up to obscene heights of power—all online with your friends.

A seismic shift in the business model of gaming was buried in this incredible adventure. MMOs were not self-contained experiences. A boxed copy of the game did not include everything needed to play. MMOs required that their persistent, digital worlds persist *somewhere*. And that somewhere was on a server.

This minor technical hurdle introduced a significant financial challenge for MMO publishers. Maintaining those servers cost money. They had to be housed, inspected, and repaired. More importantly, they had to constantly shuttle data back and forth across the infantile internet, itself costly in an era of metered connections. If gamers kept playing MMOs, they would cost the publisher more and more money. Thankfully, publishers were able to turn to a proven business model for these types of services: *subscriptions* (the S of our BAMS framework).

With MMOs, video games ceased monetizing as one-time sales, and instead became recurring revenue streams. Now gamers bought both a boxed copy at $59.99 and paid a monthly fee somewhere between $9.99 and $14.99 to access the service. This meant the longer you played, the more valuable you were to a publisher. Now a game's lifetime appeal mattered, not just its initial sales.

This shift in financial incentives subtly, but completely, changed how games were designed. Previously, good games had to be engrossing experiences, but not indefinitely lasting ones. After all, no one buys a movie ticket expecting to be able to watch the same film for years. Games were viewed in much the same way: as disposable entertainment experiences. They might take a long time to complete—sometimes hundreds of hours—but they were still finite.

In fact, because of the blades revenue model, long-lasting games were arguably financially inferior. If *Super Mario*, for example, boasted endless content, you wouldn't need to buy *Super Mario* 2. That would be terrible for an industry built around selling new games.

But subscriptions changed the game (pun intended). Publishers looked at MMO pricing and noticed that at $14.99 a month, it only took a few months of subscription revenue to equal the sale of a whole new game. Convincing people to play an MMO for four extra months seemed a lot easier—and less risky—than concepting, coding, producing, distributing, and marketing an entirely new game.

Games as a Service (GaaS) was born when publishers realized games didn't need to be static experiences. Taking advantage of the nascent internet, content updates could be pushed to constantly improve and refine titles. And these new additions would extend the shelf life of the game, garnering more subscription cash. Suddenly publishers were incentivized to create non-disposable games in order to be able to monetize them for as long as possible.

As a result, game developers began designing for permanence. The dream became to make a game so good users would never want to stop playing, because that game would never stop making money. And enduring game design is critical to the foundation of esports. Because for sports to be sports, they must stick around.

Imagine if sports cycled annually, like cartridge games did before MMOs. How could athletes train, or stadia be built, or broadcast rights be valuable if a game lasted for only a single year? Stability is required for sports, and the subscription business model brought stability to games.

So starting in 1996, there were now two ways for game developers to make money: The old way, by selling one-time fixed content (cartridges) for a fixed price, ideally as part of a console ecosystem to lockout competition (the blades monetization model). And the new way, by selling a recurring online service, for a recurring fee, for as long as possible (the subscription monetization model).

But which publisher would best take advantage of this new revenue model, and thereby shape the evolution of the gaming industry?

One of the most significant development to all esports was not an esport at all.

On November 23, 2004, the MMO *World of Warcraft* (WoW) launched from Blizzard Entertainment (now Activision Blizzard), and gaming changed forever.

WoW was superficially an improved *EverQuest*. It had better graphics, more refined gameplay systems, and more responsive controls. So why did *WoW* overshadow all competitors to conquer the MMO market?

To understand *WoW*'s success, you first need to understand the psychology of the game itself. Imagine downloading *World of Warcraft* for the first time. You design your character from myriad options, settling on a human mage before embarking on your first quest: to slay the wolves of Goldshire.[3] Your lupine massacre rewards you with valuable treasure, a level-up, and new magic. You spend some time trying out your new abilities and items before departing on your next adventure: storming the stronghold of the Defias Brotherhood of thieves. But because this quest is more difficult, the game requires you to collaborate with like-minded, low-level heroes. So you type "LFG" (looking for group) into your chat bar and quickly form an adventuring party. Together you tactically battle the Brotherhood, even becoming friends with your party's priest, who cleverly follows your lead in combat.

And because this is all tons of fun, you keep playing. Your character gains more and more levels, unlocking better and better equipment. Your proficiency with the game system increases as you continually learn and master new sorceries. And most importantly, you gain another new friend, then twelve, then two dozen as quests require more heroes to conquer higher difficulties. Eventually you form a guild—a phenomenon of the early 2000s—organizing for massive sixty-person dungeon raids against incredibly challenging world bosses.

And although you may not realize it, you are caught in the spider's web.

Because now imagine a new MMO comes out, and this new MMO is just like *World of Warcraft*, but slightly better in every way. Let's call this new MMO "WOWER." Do you switch? Do you stop playing *WoW*, and enjoy this new, better title from a competing publisher?

No, you don't. Because in WOWER you start from scratch. You don't have any of the legendary equipment you worked for hundreds (and sometimes thousands) of hours to pillage in *WoW*. You can't impress new players with the incredible aura of Thunderfury, Blessed Blade of the Windseeker—the most powerful in-game artifact—which you proudly display on every trip to the auction house in Orgrimmar to a legion of adoring fans.[4] In WOWER, you begin with nothing, just like every other new player. And that sucks.

But you don't switch for many other reasons. You don't switch to WOWER because you'd have to unlock and learn all the new game systems and abilities, and you've already built extreme tactical proficiency with *WoW* combat. You understand exactly when to polymorph an opposing rogue for a strategic bandaging, and where to blink on the battlefields of Warsong Gulch to avoid falling through the world itself. This intuitive mastery is deeply satisfying; it is a skill you are proud of and can publicly display, as you confidently carry your friends to victory in challenging player-versus-player combat, proving your hard-earned battle skills against real human foes.

And those friends. They are the most important part. You don't switch to WOWER because your friends don't play WOWER, and your guild doesn't exist in WOWER. The alliances and antagonists, the bannermen and bitter betrayals, all the rich social history you've built across hundreds of hours of digital adventure and idle chat vanish into the ether the moment you swap games.

WOWER may be a better game *objectively*, but it's not better *subjectively*. It's not better for *you*.

So despite WOWER being a better game than *WoW*, you don't play it. And WOWER vanishes into the trash bin of history. A greater game laid low by what economists term "switching costs." Because you have invested into *WoW*, and that investment is not transferable. There is a cost for switching—giving up everything you have built in Azeroth—and for you (and everyone else) the cost is unacceptably high.

So what if a few years pass, and an even better competitor to *WoW* comes out—we'll call this game "WOWEST." And WOWEST is not just better, but *a lot* better in every way. WOWEST has taken advantage of all the latest technological improvements and game design innovations to make a truly cutting-edge MMO. Surely WOWEST now stands a chance against *WoW*?

Nope. Because economists describe another factor that benefits *WoW*: network effects. Essentially, the more people that play *WoW*, the better *WoW* becomes.

Imagine it this way: The more gamers online in *WoW*, the more friendships you naturally form. The faster you gather an adventuring party or find a buyer for a rare magical item. The more guilds you compete with. And the bigger the audience you have for those Thunderfury strolls through Orgrimmar.

But most importantly, these network effects extend *outside* the game of *WoW*. Because its millions of gamers are expressing their devotion not just by playing. They are also *producing* content, from stats websites to video guides and text tutorials. They are *congregating*, in out-of-game chatrooms, real-life meet ups, and even large-scale conventions. And they are *affiliating* through tattoos, clothing, and customized gear that displays their loyalty to the Lich King (or other preferred, Azerothian fantasy faction).

WOWEST may be an incredible game. But at this point being an incredible game is not enough. *WoW* has built a rich community, making the game harder and harder to leave. Because at the end of the day people are social animals, and so society itself becomes a black hole, its intractable pull impossible to escape.

With *WoW*, we have solidification of our third SCAR factor: community. For arguably the first time ever, game worlds truly reached beyond the game itself to create a self-reinforcing society.

And community is also why *WoW* defeated *EverQuest*, *Asheron's Call*, and all the other aspirant MMOs. Blizzard understood that the key to unlocking the power of the new subscription monetization model was to build its game's community as quickly and broadly as possible. As a result, Blizzard made three key business decisions.

First, *World of Warcraft* was marketed extremely aggressively. In 2004, Blizzard was already a large publisher with a massive, built-in fanbase for its *Warcraft* franchise. But Blizzard reached beyond these guaranteed sales, running multimillion-dollar TV and in-theater advertising campaigns featuring celebrities like Ozzy Osbourne. Blizzard aimed to get everyone with even a minute interest in video games playing *WoW*, to build community.

Second, Blizzard designed *WoW* for ease of connectivity. *EverQuest* and its ilk were incredible experiences—if you could get them to work. But *World of Warcraft* was the first MMO to run silky smooth, on an endless variety of personal computers, and without internet connectivity hiccups. This simplicity let gamers play more easily, amplifying Blizzard's broad marketing campaign. And building community.

Third, *WoW* itself was designed with the new player experience in mind. *WoW* recognized that switching costs are weakest right when a new player signs up, and so the early hours of the game experience were tailor-made for addiction. New player starter areas, a clear early-game questing roadmap, fast initial level-ups, and quick newbie item acquisition all characterize the early levels of *WoW*. Some might call this elaborate onboarding tutorial or "first-time user experience" good game design. But *WoW*'s incredible early game also ensured that when lots of people played, lots of people also stuck around.

As a result, *World of Warcraft* rocketed past a million users in its first year—far faster than *EverQuest* had ever grown. And as soon as *WoW* had an initial stranglehold on the market, Blizzard further perfected subscriptions. Not only did they do an incredible job fostering community, but they reinvested the profits of subscription to secure this dominance.

As Blizzard Entertainment began collecting those $14.99 monthly payments, they plowed resources back into the game, producing the fastest, most aggressive content update schedule for an MMO ever. Blizzard consistently added more quests, new abilities, and greater challenges. *WoW* became a moving target of quality; with every patch the game got better, not just because more people were playing it, but because the game itself continually improved. Blizzard had mastered the subscription monetization model, and as a result, would prove impossible to dethrone.

At its peak in 2010, *World of Warcraft* boasted 12 million active players, amounting to an estimated $1.4 billion in subscription revenues alone. And true to the power of switching costs, network effects, and community, *WoW* remains the most popular MMO in the world at the time of this writing. In fact, in 2019 *WoW* even launched *WoW Classic*—an exact remake of the 2004 title before any improvements—to capture nostalgia for the original game. It became one of the highest-grossing video games of the year, despite being over fifteen years old.

This success highlights the most notable aspect of *WoW*. Not the billions of dollars in profits it has raked in, but the passion of its community that has sustained the game for decades.

WoW defines people's lives. It is a breeding ground not just for friendships, but life-changing social events. Countless marriages have originated from *WoW*'s group quests and late-night chats.[5] And perhaps more notably, many more divorces. In 2011, it was estimated *WoW* contributed to upward of 15 percent of separations in some countries.[6] That's right, about one in seven marriages may have been shattered because a spouse was spending too much time in Azeroth.

The bottom line: *World of Warcraft* was not just a new business model for gaming; it was a true virtual community. And that meant the birth of esports was just on the horizon.

CHAPTER FOUR

THE REVOLUTION IS TELEVISED

W hat if you could broadcast your entire life online? Such was the original concept behind Justin.tv, which launched in 2007 (as *WoW* continued to skyrocket in popularity) and quickly acquired funding from top venture capital firms like Y Combinator. Armed with a specially designed backpack and baseball cap, Justin.tv's titular Justin Kan proceeded to livestream his entire life, 24/7. Inspired by media like *The Truman Show*, Justin and co-founders Kyle Vogt, Michael Seibel, and Emmett Shear envisioned a world where anyone could broadcast themselves online. As YouTube was to home video, so Twitch aspired to be to home access cable.

While Justin individually attracted a lot of media attention for his unusual concept, traction for Justin.tv remained scarce even as his platform opened to other "livecasters." About a year after launch, Justin.tv finally had enough users that it made sense to introduce filters, to sort livecaster content by category.

Most content categories on Justin.tv bombed. Watching a nonexpert talk incessantly about topics like current events and technology proved boring, to say the least. But one filter category instantly captivated a special audience: gaming.

Viewers loved watching others play games, particularly those who were good at the games they played. And, perhaps more importantly, it was *far* easier to broadcast directly from a stationary PC than to jury-rig a wearable livecasting setup as Justin had done.

The gaming category exploded. By 2011, streaming games on Justin.tv became so popular, the category was spun out as its own website: Twitch.tv. By 2014, Justin.tv all but shut down as it merged into the newly christened parent company, Twitch Interactive. And Twitch grew so quickly, it became one of the fastest-growing media businesses of all time. The age of the streamer had arrived.

Big business took notice. Google took the lead, swooping in with a series of escalating—and incredibly competitive—offers to buy the business in 2014. Google saw the potential for a new channel of user-driven media, particularly if merged with its existing video service, YouTube. On July 14, it was widely reported that Google had purchased Twitch for $1 billion.[1]

Except they hadn't. At the last moment, Jeff Bezos and Amazon stole the deal, purchasing the website for $970 million in an all-cash deal. The slightly lower price tag is perhaps understandable, given that Amazon's strategic vision for the company reportedly aligned more closely with that of its founders. Rather than merging with an existing service like YouTube, Amazon saw Twitch as a standalone business.

Twitch's success accelerated with access to Amazon's deep pockets and strategic network. By 2017, Twitch reported a total of 355 billion minutes watched on its website. Astonishingly, this number increased by 58 percent in 2018 to reach 560 billion minutes watched.[2]

But what, exactly, were people watching? And how were they watching it?

The most important aspect of Twitch is where it *isn't*. You can't find Twitch on your television or in your local movie theater, despite it being one of the largest entertainment companies in the world. Twitch is a next-generation media service, delivering content exclusively online, to a millennial audience, who prefer watching on PC or mobile. It is an entirely digital-nativist experience.

Twitch's homepage is designed with digital interactivity in mind. It features a dazzling variety of highlighted channels, game-specific livestreams, and promoted events, encouraging you to explore and discover.

Once you click into a channel, you'll encounter a gregarious livestreaming gamer playing a game (usually incredibly well) and simultaneously explaining what he or she is doing. A blisteringly fast-scrolling chat window accompanies every stream, where viewers can type anything and everything (subject to moderation), talking both to each other and the streamer directly. In turn, the streamer (when they can take their eyes off the game) responds directly to the chat, calling out comments and praising (or teasing) viewers.

In one fell swoop, Twitch expanded the concept of online gaming communities, popularized by *World of Warcraft*, by merging television and social interactivity. The result is a kind of pro gamer cult of personality, where viewers celebrate, commiserate, and conflict with streamers, all interspliced into video of their favorite games. Think of streaming like the ultimate version of YouTube: what you want to watch is always happening now, and always ready for you to interact with.

But Twitch's viewership platform did something else critically important for gaming and esports, beyond creating new online communities. Twitch introduced the concept of *reward*, the fourth component of the SCAR model.

Before Twitch, pro gaming was a great hobby, but a lackluster way to make a living. Throughout the 2000s, tournaments provided the primary source of pro gamer income, but payouts remained extraordinarily low. In 2005, for example, the World Cyber Games US Championship awarded just $5,000 for first place.[3] And the chances of a total victory like this were vanishingly small. Even a string of marquee wins paid worse than minimum wage. Pro gaming was at best a side hustle, and at worst a cheat code to financial ruin.

It just didn't make sense to devote yourself to playing a video game full time. There was simply no reward.

The reason people dedicate their lives to mastering basketball or football is because there is a clearly defined system of milestone achievements. From college scholarships to minor league contracts, there are plenty of respectable outcomes for aspiring athletes. And the best of the best enjoy massive financial return. The chance of becoming the next LeBron James is vanishingly slim, but rise to his level and the compensation tops $50 million a year. Pro gaming needed a similar "pot of gold," and Twitch chat provided this astronomical payoff. But how?

As streamers rose in popularity, their Twitch chats quickly became crowded with hundreds (even thousands) of comments. To garner attention, Twitch lets users donate directly to a streamer, likely assuring their comment would be noticed and responded to. In the beginning, a variety of third-party apps facilitated this, but eventually Twitch embedded gifting into the Twitch UI, through a virtual currency called Twitch Bits.

Donations paired with another even more powerful monetization feature: subscription. On Twitch, if a viewer enjoys a streamer, they can subscribe to their channel, paying a fixed monthly fee (usually $4.99) to access a variety of perks, from private chats to custom Kappa emotes. While these perks may seem small, when you're consuming as much Twitch content as the average viewer (about two to three hours a day) these differentiators become hugely meaningful.

WHAT'S A KAPPA?

To really appreciate the nuances of Twitch, you need to understand its emotes. These are small images appearing in-line with chat that can be queued using special text commands. On Twitch, many of these emotes are unique to each channel, set by the host as a reward for subscribing. However, the Kappa emote is largely universal. It is a miniature picture of Josh DeSeno's face, who was an early employee of Justin.tv. Josh chose the name Kappa for his emote as a non-sequitur reference to a monster from Japanese folklore. And Twitch's viewership embraced it, in part because of Josh's early and active involvement in the community.[4]

Today, Kappa is used about one million times every day on Twitch. Its meaning is highly varied and context-dependent. It's most commonly used to praise streamers or to encourage them to try harder. However, when recolored or otherwise visually altered, Kappa can take on a huge variety of meanings. For example, a popular rainbow version celebrates pride and inclusion. Kappa is a unique part of Twitch culture, and a fun footnote to understanding modern gaming.

The impact of these donations and subscriptions cannot be understated. For the first time ever, aspiring pro gamers had a way to earn revenue without winning a major tournament. By broadcasting themselves on Twitch, they could start to acquire—slowly at first, but building over time—a loyal following of fans, each donating $1.99 here or paying a $4.99 monthly subscription there. These donations and subscriptions added up quickly. "It doesn't take that many subscribers," explains Vincent "Deathsie" Chu, a newly minted midsized streamer, "to reach a respectable level of income. At just five hundred, you are earning above minimum wage. It's not easy to achieve, but once you're there you feel the journey was worth it. I find fulfillment in watching my progress build day by day, fan by fan."

And popular streamers boast way more than 500 subscribers. By 2017, a top streamer might command 50,000 monthly paying fans or more. That means significant income: $3 million or more annually.

And critically, Twitch income is reliable. Because subscriptions are collected monthly, gaming success no longer depends on spiking a lucky series of victories at major tournaments. Twitch provides a steady income, all generated by doing what you already love—playing video games—and sharing that joy with others.

It gets better. Twitch doesn't just pay users through donations and subscriptions. The Twitch channel itself is a media platform, allowing advertisers and sponsors to access the millions of eyeballs watching popular streamers. Brands can purchase rotating ad units or buy shout-out endorsements at strategic moments, adding more fuel to the pro gaming monetization fire. At first, the brands sponsoring streams remained small and endemic. But as the reality of Twitch's audience size dawned on marketers, sponsorships exploded. Soon intergenerational brands desperate to reach a millennial audience, like Coke and BMW, joined gaming natives like Razer.

Today a top streamer can earn $10 million or more, every year, just from branded advertisements. Add to this the subscription income, donations, and other ancillary revenue sources (like repackaging historical stream highlights for YouTube), and a top streamer can earn an annual income of $25 million or more.

Becoming a pro gamer now had serious financial incentives attached, plus another type of reward: fame.

Because top streamers are watched by tens or even hundreds of thousands of viewers simultaneously, they become celebrities. They aren't just wealthy, they're iconic. The millennial equivalent of pinball wizards.

NINJA

Perhaps the most iconic celebrity streamer is Tyler "Ninja" Blevins. Beyond earning a reported $30 million a year gaming, Ninja enjoys broad fame in popular culture. He's appeared in a Super Bowl ad, signed a multibook deal, and has become the face of dozens of sponsoring brands with his uniquely dyed hair and brightly labeled headband.

But more importantly, Blevins's rise is a microcosm for gaming as a whole. Ninja started as a pro in 2009 playing *Halo 3*. Over the next eight years, he eked out a living across various titles, until a chance swap to *Fortnite* coincided with that game's rocketing popularity. Almost overnight, Ninja exploded, going from 500,000 followers in late 2017 to over 5 million by early 2018.[5]

Ninja's watershed moment was when hip-hop artist Drake, himself a huge fan, appeared on the stream, breaking Twitch's concurrent viewership record

with 635,000 fans watching and interacting simultaneously in chat. This milestone cemented Ninja as the most marketable pro gamer in history.

Tyler "Ninja" Blevins. Arguably the most famous esports celebrity alive today.

The enormous success of Twitch led the giants of Silicon Valley to take notice. Facebook entered the fray by launching Fb.gg, a livestreaming service directly integrated into personal pages, allowing everyone to share their gaming with friends. Backed by a marquee partnership with Blizzard, Facebook became the first streaming solution to offer seamless and direct games integration.

Alongside Fb.gg, YouTube promoted livestreaming under the YouTube Gaming brand, eventually inking its own exclusive deal with Blizzard. And Microsoft acquired Beam, rebranding it as Mixer, to catalyze Xbox Live content creation. Fox followed, snagging a major investment in a venture-backed startup called Caffeine. As a result, streamers were poached, extracting increasingly lucrative deals by playing competing platforms against each other. Even Ninja himself quit Twitch for Mixer in late 2019. Microsoft's offer was just too good to turn down.

And esports had all the ingredients it needed to explode. The four SCAR factors had all come into being.

Games had improved to dizzying levels of complexity, requiring deep skill to master.

Rich online networks had formed around games, facilitating digital community and competition.

Games and gaming platforms had integrated into daily life through affordable consoles and ubiquitous home PCs, creating true accessibility.

And because Twitch, Mixer, and other streaming platforms provided both fame and multimillion-dollar rewards, becoming a pro gamer was worth the time.

Like a pro gaming petri dish, the SCAR factors were ready to catalyze the rise of esports. But where would this rise begin?

CHAPTER FIVE

CRAFTING WITH THE STARS

In 1993, Dennis "Thresh" Fong embarked on a journey no one had undertaken before. Starting from an unadulterated love for the first-person shooter (FPS) *Doom*, Thresh devoted himself to mastering the genre. Just sixteen years old, he competed in, and quickly dominated, the limited tournament scene available at the time.

But Thresh wouldn't cement his place in gaming history until he won one of the largest prizes offered for a competitive video game to date: a used car.

At the 1997 Red Annihilation *Quake* tournament, Thresh defeated Tom "Entropy" Kimzey in an incredible 14 to −1 show match (the −1 was achieved by Entropy's failure to secure a single kill, combined with a penalty for in-game suicide). And

SIDEBAR: WHAT IS AN FPS?

First-person shooters (FPSs) are reflex-based gun games, where you control a single character from their perspective as they roam around a battlefield and blow away the competition with increasingly powerful firearms. The FPS genre originated with early efforts such as id Software's *Hovertank 3D*, *Catacomb 3-D*, *Wolfenstein 3D* (itself a remake of a classic 2D shooter, *Castle Wolfenstein*), and Bungie's *Marathon*. But FPSs wouldn't break into mainstream popularity until 1993, with id's *Doom*, which boasted then cutting-edge 3D graphics, and for the first time, online multiplayer capabilities, allowing gamers to blast each other even when spread across the globe.

Early *Doom* local area network (LAN) parties and hosting services such as DWANGO (short for Dial-up Wide-Area Network Game Operation) laid the foundations for modern online multiplayer gaming. And this competitive scene, already popular with *Doom*, exploded with id Software's *Quake* thanks to dedicated network code that allowed gamers to seamlessly connect to (and "frag," FPS slang for destroy) each other online.

Today, FPS remains one of the most popular genres in esports, although the focus of these games has shifted from solitary free-for-alls to tightly coordinated, team-based experiences like *Counter-Strike: Global Offensive, Valorant,* and *Overwatch..*

just like that, Thresh found himself the owner of *Quake* creator John Carmack's bright red (and gently aged) Ferrari. At its time, this was the height of gaming achievement.

Everything about Thresh's victory displays how embryonic competitive gaming was in 1997. The fact that the prize was a used (albeit custom-tuned) car. The fact that the final match was so incredibly lopsided. Even the fact that the tournament itself wasn't a main event, but an E3 sideshow without dedicated spectator space. It was clear that while Thresh was an incredibly talented gamer (who fully deserves the accolades heaped on him), the gaming scene was not ready for Thresh.

But esports *was* rising. Just somewhere outside the Western world, and in an entirely new genre of game.

In 1995, Chris Metzen and James Phinney set to work developing a sequel to *Warcraft II*. The *Warcraft* franchise had been Blizzard's biggest hit at the time, single-handedly

WHAT IS AN RTS?

A real-time strategy game (RTS) is an army-management simulator typically played from a top-down, 3D isometric perspective. In an RTS, a player controls a single race or faction, which determines the production buildings they can construct and the military units they can recruit. The player then commands their armies to harvest resources, create new structures, and train new soldiers, all while battling opponents for control of the map's scarce resources. (Hence the popular RTS phrase, "We require more minerals.")

The origins of the first RTSs are arguable, with some industry sources tracing the genre's roots back to 1981, or even earlier.[1] However, most consider the RTS genre's true birth to be *Dune II*, a game adaption of the 1984 movie.[2] *Dune II* features most of the elements pivotal to RTS games, including resource harvesting, army management, and building construction.

Today, modern RTS games feature two levels of gameplay skill: micro, directing the exact attacks of individual units; and macro, managing an overall economy of resource harvesting and base construction. Pro players instantly switch between these two facets of gameplay, issuing upward of 300 commands per minute to execute perfectly orchestrated attacks. Because of the sheer number of buildings and units on screen (typically somewhere between 200 and 300), RTSs remain among of the most skill-intensive games across all of esports.

popularizing the real-time strategy (RTS) genre of video games.

Warcraft itself almost never existed. Original builds were based off Warhammer, the popular tabletop wargame by Games Workshop. But a failure to secure commercial terms with Games Workshop left Blizzard to launch *Warcraft* as an original intellectual property (IP) franchise.

Despite (or perhaps because of) this fraught history with the company, Metzen and Phinney continued looking to Games Workshop for inspiration; in particular their popular science fiction brand Warhammer 40,000. Unafraid to loot the game's universe for its best ideas and brightest points of innovation, the two designers set about crafting arguably the greatest RTS of all time.

Released in March of 1998, *StarCraft* was special right from the get-go. The game boasted cutting-edge graphics, but flexible system requirements across both Windows and Macintosh platforms (though the Macintosh version launched slightly later). It told a deeply engaging and incredibly creative tale of interstellar war (introducing notable characters like Sarah Kerrigan, the corrupted human psychic). But it also brought two incredible innovations to the RTS genre.

The first innovation was asymmetric factions. Previously, RTS games achieved competitive balance by forcing players to use roughly the same composition of units and buildings. Gamers might be able to make limited choices about their faction, but these differences proved largely cosmetic.

StarCraft threw this limitation out the window, instead featuring three distinct races: Terran (power-armored humans supported by intergalactic battle cruisers); Protoss (psychic aliens that could teleport with the power of crystals); and Zerg (mutated monsters overrunning civilization at the direction of their hive mind). Each race played uniquely, with their own buildings and battlefield mechanics. Perhaps more importantly, the races were almost perfectly balanced. Whether you picked Protoss for their invisible Dark Templar, or Terran for their nuclear missiles, each race was evenly matched against the others. This made gameplay fun and diverse, raising the skill ceiling for an RTS as never before.

More importantly, this variety introduced a sense of deep personalization. Your favorite race really mattered. You weren't just a *StarCraft* player. You were a Protoss pro or a Zerg queen.

· *StarCraft*'s other big innovation, and arguably its most important, was the integration of online matchmaking. In 1996, Blizzard launched Battle.net, the first-ever in-game platform to allow gamers to directly challenge each other. Systems to sync gamers had already existed, but Battle.net was the first to make competitive matching truly seamless. By directly building Battle.net into the game client, intense head-to-head battles were suddenly not a series of LAN codes and painfully slow loads away, but an instant experience activated with a single, in-game mouse click.

Blizzard doubled down on this multiplayer aspect by including a "spawn" feature. Now anyone with a friend who owned *StarCraft* could install a limited, multiplayer-only version on their computer and battle online with millions of other gamers for free, vastly increasing *StarCraft*'s accessibility.

As a result, *StarCraft* became Battle.net's flagship game. And *StarCraft*'s combination of high-skill gameplay, accessible system requirements, instantaneous community, and free access via spawning created a global gaming phenomenon. In the year of its release, *StarCraft* became the best-selling PC game of all time, moving an incredible 1.5 million copies.[3] Over the next decade, *StarCraft* sold millions more units around the globe, about half in South Korea.

You may be wondering why a country not even among the twenty-five most populous in the world would buy *half* the copies of a popular video game.

South Korea has always been a relatively unique nation, from fraught relations with its northern neighbor to an unusual economy dominated by domestic super-companies (called chaebol). But in terms of catalyzing esports, South Korea had two very important things going for it. First was an incredibly high density of high-speed internet connections, making it "the most wired nation on earth."[4] Second was an extremely concentrated population, with about half of all South Koreans living in the capital city of Seoul, many of whom were underemployed as a result of the 1997 Asian financial crisis.

The extreme density of living conditions in Seoul created opportunities for some unusual types of business. Seeking what we would now call a "third place" to unwind from the home or office, the ubiquity of cheap internet led to the rise of so-called "PC bangs," roughly translated as gaming cafés or LAN centers (but literally, "PC rooms"). PC bangs provided an escape from the stresses of Korean society, particularly the brutally long corporate work hours (which ranked anywhere between No. 1 and No. 3 in the world) or the grueling preparations for college entrance exams.[5] Clientele could relax, order coffee and even food, and escape into the fantasy world of gaming with a like-minded community of aficionados.

And the game of choice in PC bangs quickly became *StarCraft*.

So, far ahead of the rest of the world, the SCAR factors required for esports came into existence in South Korea. Domestic telecommunications infrastructure provided accessibility, PC bangs created community, and *StarCraft* brought skill.

But what about the reward?

In South Korea, there had always been some social benefits to being good at gaming, whether through message board credibility or leaderboard cache. But crucially, this status was always intangible. Always online.

PC bang culture created real-life gaming celebrities. "Since everyone played *StarCraft*, developing a high level of skill brought true social cachet," explains Dr. Joseph Ahn, the lead trade and financial economist at the United States Office of Management and Budget. "You were champion of your PC bang. You represented your home turf in a digital battlefield raging across Korea, every night. And this in turn made many players think, 'How far could I go?'"

In a way, PC bang culture mirrored English pinball halls or Californian arcades. But unlike these antecedents, the digitally interconnected and population-dense city of Seoul created intense network effects. "PC bangs were on every block. An entire generation of kids grew up playing *StarCraft*, discussing strategy, showing off their skills after school, and organizing tournaments," Ahn explains.

Gaming had found its first payoff, albeit a social one. But in the uniquely insular economy of South Korea, that success would quickly translate into monetary gain.

Lim "BoxeR" Yo-hwan dominated the South Korean PC bang scene, coming to be called "The Emperor of Terran." As *StarCraft*'s popularity birthed a national tournament industry— KPGA, Starleague, WGC, and more—BoxeR won them all. His highest achievements include winning the WGC Championship not once, but twice, and earning the coveted title of the first "bonjwa": the undisputed best player in the world.

But most importantly, BoxeR didn't win these tournaments at some E3 tradeshow. He won them on national television. The popularity of *StarCraft*, and the low cost to televise the competitions, led to the foundation of networks like Ongamenet (OGN), which quickly secured domestic broadcasting deals— at first as specialist media, but eventually as mainstream television.

BoxeR wasn't just winning esports tournaments. He was winning them in front of the nation.

This public dominance fueled a national narrative of professional gaming. Soon BoxeR joined South Korea's biggest pro team, SK Telecom (named because of the domestic conglomerate's interest in esports). And with television rights and corporate support, prizing skyrocketed. BoxeR's lifetime winnings quickly climbed above $100,000.[6,7] Still not a fortune, but a far cry better than the used car Thresh took home in the US.

But prizing itself didn't necessarily matter to BoxeR, because he had more reliable ways to earn money: fans.

Thanks to Asia's wider (and somewhat cultish) fan club culture, BoxeR quickly amassed a devoted following of over half a million loyalists to purchase tickets, merchandise, and even DVD compilations of his greatest hits. The fan club structure was primitive, but it at least partially anticipated Twitch's subscription-reward model with its mail-in redemptions and signature events.

The rise of BoxeR's celebrity helped draw sponsors, a trend compounded by the insular nature of Korean companies, which tended to focus exclusively on domestic marketing. Consequently, Korea Airlines flared Protoss tail decals and the Korean Air Force (appealing to a younger generation bound into mandatory military service) launched their own esports pro team.

Corporate sponsorship catalyzed investment in domestic talent. For the first time, Korean esports teams developed an organized ecosystem of managers, trainers, sparring partners, and even dedicated team houses where players would eat, sleep, and practice. Eager to replicate BoxeR's success, corporations also secured team contracts with rising talent, specifying salaries, benefits, and prizing splits. A dedicated league circuit emerged to allow for a steady stream of games split across seasons, much like a physical sports league. To this day, this deep ecosystem of nurturing talent contributes to Korea's continuing dominance in esports.

And all these rewards for success amplified as *StarCraft*'s popularity magnified in the isolated bubble of South Korea. While it was still hard to earn a true living as a *StarCraft* pro in South Korea, BoxeR at least created a narrative of success for a lucky few. During the height of his career, he likely took home well over $250,000 a year.

BoxeR's financial success and national celebrity led more and more devoted *StarCraft* fans to take notice. Domestically, new legends like Flash and Jaedong emerged. And while most *StarCraft* pros remained Korean, aspiring gamers from around the world began moving to Korea to compete. Unable to garner rewards internationally, they bravely emigrated to a new home, where they couldn't speak the language, attempting to find financial compensation for their mastery. Perhaps most notable of this vanguard is Guillaume Patry, a French-Canadian *StarCraft* pro and the first-ever (and only) non-Korean winner of Starleague.

As this esports infrastructure emerged in South Korea throughout the early 2000s, Western media looked on and laughed. They viewed Korea as a microcosm of absurdity, a cautionary tale of what might happen if gaming culture were taken too far. As late as 2010, popular English-language websites published clickbait articles asking, "Why is Korea Cuckoo for *StarCraft*?"[8]

But what the rest of the world missed was that the conditions for esports to thrive were simply present first in Korea. The country wasn't strange; they were advanced. Korea only looked unique because they were first. As soon as the SCAR factors in South Korea propagated globally, the rest of the world followed their example. And with the launch of Twitch's streaming platform in North America in 2011, the isolation of Korea ended. The era of esports dawned internationally at last.

PART II
IT HAS BEGUN!

CHAPTER SIX

RIOT IN THE STREETS

E sports exploded as streaming platforms spread the celebrity and financial rewards of pro gaming around the world. But as our SCAR factors went global, would *StarCraft* replicate its success in Korea and become the first truly international esport?

No. In an ironic twist, *StarCraft* would instead incubate its biggest competitor. And this new genre of game—the massive online battle arena (MOBA)—would dethrone its parent and dominate esports.

WHAT'S A MOBA?

Massive online battle arenas (MOBAs) bear striking similarities to the RTS games they evolved from. In MOBAs, players control a champion from a top-down, 3D isometric perspective, fighting alongside four other human-controlled heroes against an opposing team of five. Each team battles over three contested areas, called "lanes," protected by a series of defensive structures. Periodically, AI-controlled minions spawn on these lanes. The minions can be killed for resources or protected to assist in "pushing" the lane, or advancing toward the opponent's home base. The ultimate objective is to breach this base and destroy the opposing team's central structure, located at the maximally distant point where all three lanes converge.

MOBAs are deceptively skill-intensive. Experienced players must manage map vision and tactical combat, which involves executing up to a dozen abilities with split-second timing. Last hitting, a popular mechanic in many MOBAs, also raises the skill ceiling by forcing players to deal the final hit to enemy minions to receive additional rewards.

StarCraft was more than just a best-selling RTS phenomenon. It also included a powerful creative tool: a map editor. This software allowed intrepid users to build their own custom battlefields, adding further replayability and depth to the already legendary RTS experience.

As amateur game designers investigated *StarCraft*'s toolset, they quickly discovered ambitious projects were possible. In particular, the map editor could be used to create role-playing games (RPGs), like Dungeons and Dragons, inside of *StarCraft*. These RPGs played like *StarCraft*—from a top-down, 3D isometric perspective—but focused on controlling only a single unit (the hero) instead of an army. While many versions of these "StarPGs" were popular, one in particular stood out: *Aeon of Strife*.

In *Aeon of Strife* (also called *Aeon Strife* or *AoS*), a central hero battles against waves of advancing enemies split across three lanes, earning resources that can be used to upgrade the hero's attack damage, shields, and more. Although the *AoS* mod was popular at the time, nobody yet understood it as the harbinger of an evolution in gaming.

But Blizzard Entertainment *was* inspired by *Aeon of Strife*. In particular, its hero-centric mechanic seemed uniquely suited to storytelling, allowing a single unit to matter more than the hundreds of cannon-fodder soldiers surrounding it.

And so, on July 3, 2002, Blizzard released a successor to *StarCraft*, *Warcraft III: Reign of Chaos*, which incorporated a hero-management feature. Previously RTS games had focused only on the clash of large armies, with no space for individualism. But *Warcraft III* kicked this convention to the curb. New heroic units leveled up, acquired gold, and purchased items, just like in traditional RPGs. And the map itself wasn't merely a static environment for battle. So-called "creeps," or neutral enemies, protected key story objectives and could be killed for resources. Both mechanics were arguably inspired by *AoS*.

As part of *Warcraft III*, these features largely served to tell stories, offering persistent protagonists that evolved across campaigns. Gamers fell in love with this rich blend of narrative and army management, and *Warcraft III* sold 1 million units in its first month, making it the fastest-selling PC game at the time.[1]

MOD? MODDER? MODDING?

To understand the evolution of MOBAs, it's important to be familiar with three very similar gaming terms: mod, modder, and modding. All are abbreviations of *modification*, because they all relate to *modifying* an existing game to create a new experience. A modder is a person who modifies games. Modding is the act of altering games, and a mod is the product of this work.

Modding is generally viewed positively by gaming communities (although not always publishers), as its outcome is a genuine creative work. But there are also more malignant ways to modify games. For example, map hacking involves altering a game's code to track other players' movements to create an unfair advantage.

And like *StarCraft* before it, *Warcraft III* shipped with a map editor tool. The core game even included in its launch files examples of how clever coders might robustly reinterpret the *Warcraft* game; for example, as a tank racing sim.

Duly inspired, map modder Eul set out to remake *Aeon of Strife* inside of *Warcraft III*. But Eul took full advantage of *Warcraft III*'s mechanical improvements. For the first time in *AoS* history, hero units could not only increase in raw mechanical power, but they could also master new abilities and shop for powerful artifacts. And because *Warcraft III* allowed for large-scale multiplayer games, Eul permitted groups of five to play against each other, battling down the map's three lanes in tense team fights. Thus, the popular mod *Defense of the Ancients* (*DotA*) was born.

Even in its embryonic form, the hallmarks of modern MOBAs were present in *DotA*: hero powers, shopping, a tri-lane battlefield, and more. The brilliance of Eul's modding is difficult to understate. *DotA* took off. While it's almost impossible to gather data on early mod popularity, it's likely as much as 10 percent of all *Warcraft III* online games involved this custom mod. For a work of amateur design, this is an incredible level of popularity.

Eul's work inspired the larger community. Copycat after copycat mod spawned and each *DotA* spin-off brought its own minor innovations—perhaps a clever reinterpretation of hero powers, or a twist on item pricing. Amateur designers Meian and RagnOr, and eventually Steve "Guinsoo" Feak, took it upon themselves to agglomerate the most popular of these disparate mods into an ultimate version: *DotA Allstars*.

Amazingly, the popularity of *Allstars* began to eclipse *Warcraft III* itself, which at this point was waning into its post-release half-life. The mod only continued to improve under the stewardship of yet another designer, IceFrog, who streamlined *DotA* into a viciously competitive experience with countless balance updates.

But for all its passionate devotees, *Allstars* also had a clear limitation: it was built entirely inside of its parent game, *Warcraft III*. This meant it relied exclusively on this game's existing assets, powers, items, and other core design choices. No matter how much the community innovated, reinterpreted, and revised, they could not fundamentally build beyond *Warcraft III*'s impressively robust, but nonetheless limited, design.

Allstars was crying out for a game publisher to notice it and breathe life into a standalone *DotA* game. And surely that publisher would be Blizzard Entertainment. After all, Blizzard was perfectly positioned to capitalize on *DotA*'s success. They arguably owned the entire game, since the mod was built exclusively with their intellectual property and game assets.

But that was not to be.

Because at the same time *DotA Allstars* rose in popularity, another game by Blizzard took over the world: *World of Warcraft*. The massive financial and cultural success of *WoW* also had a disastrous side effect, blinding Blizzard to the potential of another of its creations. How could Blizzard care about an amateur map when *WoW* was rewriting the rules of digital worlds?

WoW's success also inadvertently created another distraction: a merger with another massive games company, Activision.[2] The success of Blizzard's MMO directly led Activision to pursue and close this alliance between 2007 and 2008, drawing focus from senior leadership at both organizations.

More fundamentally, Blizzard struggled to perceive *DotA* as a threat. After all, gamers still needed to own a copy of *Warcraft III* to play the mod. Hadn't Blizzard made its map editor public

WHEN BAD DESIGN GETS GOOD

An often-cited tenet of modern game design is to "give players meaningful choices." Good games are fun to play because they present a series of interesting decisions. Therefore, it is commonly viewed as bad game design to give players non-meaningful choices, because the decisions created aren't interesting. Let's illustrate this point with two examples.

First, suppose I create a Wizardry game that lets you choose between two spells: Fireball and Lightning Bolt. Both spells have different uses. Fireball, for example, is more effective against Ice Elementals. But Lightning Bolt is better against Robots. The choice between Fireball and Lightning Bolt is meaningful, because each spell is uniquely valuable. This is considered good game design.

In contrast, suppose Wizardry presented you with a choice between Fireball and Stronger Fireball. Technically the game presents a decision, but it's a false one. This is commonly considered bad game design, because Stronger Fireball is just better than Fireball in every way.

However, what many modern game designers miss is that sometimes false choices are powerful tools to quickly engage new players. For example, suppose Wizardry asks you to pick between two spells again: Fireball and Acid Blast. After playing for an hour, you realize Acid Blast is stronger than Fireball because few enemies resist Acid damage. Technically, the choice between Acid Blast and Fireball is just like the choice between Fireball and Stronger Fireball; optimizable, and hence false.

But does this decision really feel this way to the player? Many gamers might feel a sense of mastery, not frustration, at this choice. Because after playing Wizardry, they have learned that Acid Blast is better. Demonstrable mastery has been gained. After all, only newbies take Fireball.

League of Legends (*LoL*) is particularly good at employing false choices—technically bad game design—to powerful effect. *LoL* features an item shop with literally millions of possible combinatorial choices. However, for each hero, only a few item builds are viable, and these are easily searched online. Thus, among newer players, mastering itemization becomes a quick way to improve right out of the gate.

In esports, both accessibility and skill matter. And false-choice design can go a long way to making a game feel accessible, even if it ultimately doesn't contribute much to the skill required to play.

in the hopes of exactly this happening, of a community-driven map spurring incremental sales of its parent game?

Finally, Blizzard had a cultural problem. The company arguably made the best video games in the world, and that success bred arrogance. How could gaming innovation come from outside Blizzard's walls? DotA, and MOBA mods in general, were often perceived as being simplified RTS games. After all, they only focused on one unit per player and were played on only a single map. Surely that meant they were more primitive experiences that required less skill to play?

What Blizzard missed was that DotA's supposed simplicity was also a massive design advantage. The focus on a single hero unit made DotA easy to pick up and instantly fun to play, and this streamlining belied incredible complexity. While controlling one hero in DotA was *simpler* than controlling an army of hundreds in StarCraft, it turned out it wasn't *easier*. Players still had to target each ability pixel-perfectly, position for surprise ambushes ("ganks"), and itemize their hero by last-hitting AI-controlled creeps.

DotA proved a deeply skill-intensive game.

Previously, we've discussed each element of SCAR as a universal good—the more the better, so to speak. Grow community or increase rewards, and esports' potential further catalyzes. But two SCAR factors are often, but not always, negatively correlated: skill and accessibility.

As a game's skill increases, so too does the difficulty of learning its mechanical systems. In turn, increases in skill frequently cascade deleteriously into the new player experience as added complexity results in newbies feeling overwhelmed, confused, or discouraged. Accessibility is reduced.

As a new player in StarCraft or Warcraft, it's hard to control 200 units and a network of bases all at once. Over time it becomes fun and incredibly rewarding, but first-time players might find it stressful and confusing. You can't remember what you built where, and you don't notice your armies getting attacked until it's too late. There is just too much happening at once. You don't understand what you're doing wrong or how to improve. Even though the game looks fun, you aren't enjoying it. So you quit. The skill-intensiveness of the RTS drives you away.

The inverse relationship between skill and accessibility also holds. If a game is too easy to learn, a reduction in skill is often the root cause. I can teach you the rules of tic-tac-toe quickly, but it's not a particularly deep game. Accessibility and skill must be naturally balanced against each other.

Blizzard completely missed that *DotA*'s single-hero focus made it significantly more accessible than RTS games, without sacrificing too much skill. As a result, MOBAs were structurally positioned to be stronger esports.

So if Blizzard didn't capture the MOBA market, who did?

An incredible seven years after the launch of *Warcraft III*, the first standalone commercial MOBA, *Demigod*, came to market in 2009.

For the first time, MOBA gamers didn't need to rely on a map hack in a nearly decade-old title. And *Demigod*'s standalone retail launch was buoyed by a triple-A developer, Gas Powered Games (GPG). Founded by design legend Chris Taylor, GPG already had the successful *Dungeon Siege* franchise under its belt. *Demigod*'s timing was near perfect, coming to market just as Twitch was taking off. But sometimes fate intervenes.

A mistimed launch with retailer GameStop in 2009 caused massive technical problems. Eager gamers couldn't battle each other online because *Demigod*'s servers hadn't been switched on. Early negative press spiraled, and instead of benefiting from the early days of livestreaming, *Demigod* suffered. The few eager launch day broadcasters discovered an unplayable game.

Demigod never recovered from the cycle of bad press. Although there was a lot to love under the surface, Chris Taylor's forgotten masterpiece would be relegated to the dustbin of history.

The MOBA crown had yet to be claimed. So who would try to seize it next?

Guinsoo, the intrepid map hacker from the original *DotA* community, had joined a new company: Riot Games. At this point, Riot was just an upstart developer with no proven pedigree other than a passion for the MOBA genre. Founded by USC roommates Brandon Beck and Marc Merrill, Riot set out to create a faithful clone of *DotA Allstars*, but freed from the shackles of *Warcraft III*.

And with Guinsoo's help, *League of Legends* (*LoL*), the modern-day titan of esports, was born.

Launching in October 2009, *LoL* featured everything Guinsoo had loved about his original *DotA* mod—multiple heroes, tri-lane pushes, last-hitting creeps, and customizable itemization—all built from the ground up to deliver a best-in-class, standalone experience.

There was just one problem. *LoL* wasn't alone. At almost the same time, S2 Games launched their own *DotA* clone: *Heroes of Newerth* (*HoN*). And S2 enjoyed many structural advantages over Riot. The developer had been around since 2003, having previously launched the commercially successful *Savage*. And six years of development experience translated into quality: at launch, *HoN* was arguably a much better game.

HoN wasn't the only contender coming down the pike. Another legendary game developer, Valve Software, of *Half-Life* fame, had also noticed the success of *DotA Allstars* and invited IceFrog to join them. At this point, IceFrog and Guinsoo were embroiled in a personal battle of criticism and blame, as each asserted the other's exploitation of *DotA* assets for personal benefit. Whatever the underlying truth, IceFrog found himself spearheading Valve's MOBA project. And in addition to being crafted by a marquee publisher, Valve's game appeared the heir apparent for another reason: It had inherited the *DotA* brand and was christened *Dota* 2.

The battle for the future of MOBAs had begun.

When *League of Legends* debuted in late 2009, its publisher, Riot Games, made a critical pricing choice. *LoL* launched as part of an emerging breed of free-to-play (F2P) games.

In the West, F2P monetization was driven by the growing popularity of mobile games (although the model had been used successfully across Asia for years). In an F2P title, the initial download or installation is entirely free. Instead of making money on game sales, the publisher instead earns income from incremental, in-game purchases. These digital items can range from material in-game benefits (like extra lives) to purely cosmetic upgrades (like new costumes).

In-game purchases are called microtransactions because the game purchase has been split from one high-priced, single-time sale into numerous smaller transactions. And *microtransactions* are the M in our BAMS framework.

In many ways, microtransactions are a modernized interpretation of the console industry's razor-and-blades pricing. But now the "razor" is the game itself, and the "blades" are digital downloads. And because digital downloads have almost zero incremental cost, the need to charge an upfront price for the razor disappears. As a result, the accessibility of F2P games is extremely high. After all, they are free!

Riot Games didn't invent microtransactions, but they were one of the first publishers to introduce the concept to esports. And microtransactions were crucial in securing Riot's victory in the MOBA war, because the game's potential player base wasn't artificially restricted by an upfront fee.

In contrast, *HoN* launched on May 12, 2010, as a regularly priced game. As a result, *HoN* constantly struggled to attract the same critical mass of users as *LoL*. *LoL* quickly built a larger community than *HoN*, jumpstarting the same cycle of network effects and switching costs that protected *World of Warcraft*: more fan content, greater social credibility, faster matchmaking, and more. All facilitated by community.

And just like *WoW*, these advantages translated into more money for Riot. While *HoN* made $59.99 up front with every game sale, Riot earned about ten dollars with each new Champion purchased. And players weren't just buying one or two heroes but dozens, turning *LoL*'s F2P model into a cash cow.

As a result, *LoL* forced *HoN* to copy its F2P model in 2011, just a year after launch. But the damage was already done. By 2012, Riot boasted 12 million active players, while *HoN* struggled with a disastrous account breach.[3] And soon after, *Heroes of Newerth* began the inglorious process of gradual shutdown.

By now, Riot's success was widely imitated. It seemed every week brought announcements of upcoming competition: from FPS MOBAs like *Monday Night Combat* to Turbine Studio's DC Comics–branded *Infinite Crisis*. Even major mobile publishers like Zynga joined the fray with the ill-remembered *Solstice Arena*. But all these games would struggle against the network effects and switching costs first spurred by Riot's microtransactions.

But Riot had yet to confront its biggest challenger. *Dota 2* had been in development for over three years, and when the game launched in 2013, there was a palpable sense that a real contender to the crown had arrived. And *Dota 2* would, in fact, prove the first (and only) commercially successful MOBA after *LoL*. But not because *Dota 2* was a very good game (although it is), or because it bore the *DotA* legacy. But again because of its implementation of a BAMS monetization model.

Valve had studied and learned from *HoN*'s disintegration. The publisher knew that for *Dota 2* to stand a chance, their game had to address the switching costs of the MOBA genre.

So at launch, *Dota 2* wasn't just another microtransaction-monetized game. It also became the first MOBA to make not just the game itself but also every single one of its heroes free-to-play—further improving accessibility. Not only that, but *DotA*'s gameplay hewed exceptionally closely to *LoL*—so much so that the titles required almost identical skill sets. Both decisions made switching from *LoL* to *Dota 2* easier.

And *Dota 2* made a third, critical choice. The game became the first MOBA to tie its monetization model directly into the rewards for playing. The more cosmetic items and other digital improvements *DotA* fanatics purchased, the higher the prizing for *DotA* tournaments. This not only created a community incentive for gamers to spend, but also fueled astronomically high payouts. To date, *Dota 2* remains the best-prized esport, with its recent 2019 Invitational breaking $30 million.[4]

Dota 2 offered a credible challenge to *LoL*, not just because it was a well-designed game but because it innovated its monetization model to improve accessibility and foster community.

Today, *Dota 2* remains the second most popular MOBA in the world, earning Valve tens of millions each month in profit.[5] It has also evolved into arguably the most skill-intensive esport in the world, further cementing its strategic differentiation.

Given all these competitive successes, by 2012 even Blizzard had accepted the importance of MOBAs. And so the company that had arguably birthed the genre in the first place at last threw its hat into the ring, plowing ahead with development of its own challenger title. But the massively entrenched communities of existing competitors made prospects grim from the outset.

Worse, Blizzard had somehow *lost* its claim to the *DotA* brand, despite *DotA* originating inside a Blizzard game. In May of 2012, Blizzard had settled a longstanding lawsuit, allowing Valve to keep the rights to the *DotA* name.[6] Had Blizzard acted earlier, it's almost certain they would have controlled the brand.[7]

Blizzard continued development regardless. Hoping to borrow some pedigree from the original *DotA Allstars* mod, the company rebranded its MOBA entrant *Blizzard All-Stars*. And Blizzard identified several genre gaps to exploit with their title. Crucially, both *Dota 2* and *LoL* lacked story-driven characters. Blizzard hoped that leveraging their beloved heroes—from *StarCraft*, *Warcraft*, and *Diablo*—would win the hearts and minds of gamers. *Dota 2*, in particular, was vulnerable to IP differentiation, with characters like Sniper and Axe named for their abilities, and not their personalities.

Furthermore, Blizzard noticed that many of the mechanics in MOBAs were of questionable design value. For example, last-hitting remained an integral part of both *LoL*'s and *Dota 2*'s gameplay, even though this feature began life as a legacy quirk of how *Warcraft III* assigned experience. *Dota 2* had even leaned into this mechanic, allowing players to last-hit their own minions to deny opponents' gold. Blizzard felt that even though this was a skill-intensive mechanic, removing it would modernize and streamline MOBA gameplay. Similarly, they opted to remove item builds from the game to prevent false optimization choices.

And so, on June 2, 2015, after yet another rebrand, the newly christened *Heroes of the Storm* launched.

It was a train wreck from day one. Because the market gaps Blizzard identified for its MOBA were not real market gaps. As we have seen, esports thrive on SCAR factors. Introducing story-driven characters does nothing, and reducing skill is a net negative.

Worse, Blizzard didn't learn from the success of *DotA*. It did not implement a monetization model that could fight against network effects and switching costs. Instead, Blizzard opted for an exact copy of *LoL*'s free-to-play store.

Heroes of the Storm was dead on arrival.

Today, *Heroes of the Storm* is a valuable lesson to other esports because there is a fundamental and terrifying truth at the heart of its failure: it is a good game. *Heroes of the Storm* features best-in-class hero mechanics alongside a richly polished game engine. The title remains fun to play, even to this day. But in esports, great doesn't cut it. Unless a game amplifies SCAR factors or improves BAMS monetization, it can't compete. It took a few years to admit defeat, but by late 2018 Blizzard officially killed *Heroes of the Storm* esports.[8]

And while Blizzard designed for failure, Riot evolved esports yet again. As *LoL*'s fanbase surged toward 100 million devotees, Riot set about creating a unified competitive ecosystem.

To do so, they made smart but counterintuitive choices—like deleting popular game modes, such as the Crystal Scar map of the Dominion mode—to standardize *LoL*'s gameplay. But most importantly, Riot created a publisher-sanctioned league for *LoL* events.

In August 2012, Riot announced the League of Legends Championship Series (LCS). Inspired by Korean *StarCraft* tournaments, the LCS was a closed ecosystem, using relegation to cycle top teams who competed for millions in prizing. And with this master stroke, Riot's MOBA now began to have more in common with soccer or baseball than *Warcraft III*. A true sport was coming into being. Or at least, an enduring competitive experience.

The LCS grew and grew. From streamlined production values to dedicated hosts to pro-player video profiles, the LCS became the first esports league to introduce premium production to the West. And critically, the LCS enhanced the reward of playing *LoL*. It created a true pro structure to aspire to and for amateur fans to marvel at.

Now the esports event that opened this book—*League of Legends'* 2013 World Championships at the Los Angeles Staples Center—is placed in its full context. The tournament that rocketed esports into the public consciousness was not a fluke, but the natural consequence of the gaming industry's decades-long evolution.

And Blizzard watched it all from the shadows. Had Riot won the war? Had an upstart publisher unseated gaming's goliath? Or would *League of Legends* prove a painful lesson to the publisher—one that bred not only suffering, but learning?

Rather than admit defeat, Blizzard prepared to strike back at Riot, orchestrating a vengeful coup to steal back the crown of esports.

CHAPTER SEVEN
WATCHING OVER US

Blizzard began developing a game under the codename Project Titan in early 2008. The top-secret project aimed to accomplish two strategic objectives: to leapfrog *World of Warcraft* to become the next great MMO, and to create an entirely new IP for Blizzard.

Over the next five years, Titan took shape as a class-based, massive multiplayer shooter. Set on a near-future Earth, players traded across a robust economy during the day and engaged in sci-fi warfare at night.

Sounds cool for sure, but the game was a mess. Though it's unclear exactly what went wrong. Varying accounts claim a vision too ambitious, a development timetable too undefined, and a core gameplay loop that proved too unwieldy to balance. Whatever the final cause, Blizzard continued dumping resources into the game, year after year, and Titan only got worse and worse.

The project received its official cancellation in the fall of 2013. Most of the development team moved on, but a skeleton crew remained, tasked with salvaging something from the ashes of a failed $50 million development cycle.[1]

Morale was low. Blizzard had canceled games before, but never such a high-profile project. Yet Titan's remaining team were eager to reclaim their reputations. They quickly noticed the best part of Titan was its shooting mechanics. Focusing on that, within a few weeks the holdouts turned around an FPS prototype. Titan's heroic powers gave their demo a compelling twist compared to the more realistic shooters of the time, like *Counter-Strike*. Out of the ashes of failure, a new project was greenlit. And *Overwatch* was born.

An identity quickly emerged for the self-described "hero shooter," with a brightly animated style, optimistic tone, and compellingly diverse cast of superpowered characters battling across near sci-fi Earth. After its official announcement at BlizzCon 2014, *Overwatch* progressed rapidly, beginning closed beta testing in 2015. An open beta test shortly thereafter raked in an incredible 10 million players.[2] By *Overwatch*'s May 2016 release date, gamers were ravenous for Blizzard's spectacular new IP.

Overwatch exploded, reaching 40 million players within two years, a feat almost unequaled at the time.[3] But what explains *Overwatch*'s success? It wasn't incredibly well-designed mechanics, loveable characters, or a near-perfect level of polish. The answer is much simpler. What makes *Overwatch* notable to the history of esports is not its gameplay, but its revenue model.

Up until 2014, esports games made money using three of the four BAMS models: blades, subscription, and (more recently) microtransactions. All these revenue models make a critical assumption, which we'll call the game-first paradigm (GFP).

In the GFP, the whole point of esports is to drive sales of the game behind the sport. Think of Riot and their successful LCS tournament structure. The LCS was so successful because it galvanized the *LoL* community to play more—and hence spend more—on the game.

In the GFP, esports are effectively a marketing expense, funded by the publisher and recouped through incremental sales. They are almost extensions of the blades or microtransaction revenue models in that an upfront sacrifice produces longer-term benefits.

But the GFP misses the point. It's like the NFL hosting football games to sell footballs: silly. When we think of the NFL, we imagine much more than pigskins. We think of stadiums filled with spectators, roaring crowds, the Super Bowl, and, of course, those Super Bowl commercials. We think of the NFL not as a league designed to promote playing football, but as an entertainment experience in and of itself.

It was this insight that led Nate Nanzer, then Blizzard's global director of research and consumer insights, to begin promoting a new worldview for esports. Looking at *LoL* and its LCS success, Nate (and many others at Blizzard) saw a vehicle for selling not just games, but entertainment. And that entertainment could be inherently valuable, independent of the game it promoted.

And so, the entertainment-first paradigm (EFP) was born. Under the EFP, esports are not a cost center or a marketing expense. They are a standalone business capable of generating revenues in and of themselves. It's great that esports help sell games, just like it's great that NFL matches sell footballs. But it's not the reason for being. Sports exist first as media properties: selling franchises, sponsorships, broadcasting rights, and more. And esports are no different.

And so at BlizzCon 2016, the halls of the Anaheim Convention Center erupted in rapturous applause as this new paradigm was unveiled to the world with the introduction of the Overwatch League (OWL). This event may be the single most important day in the history of all esports. In one fell swoop, celebrities, traditional sports franchise owners, esports teams, and even Elon Musk met with Activision Blizzard in closed-door sessions. The result was the first-ever esports franchise sales pitch, and a web of networks and relationships that would catalyze the growth of most of the industry's major teams.

FIRST TO FRANCHISE

It is arguable that Riot Games understood the value of the EFP model even before Blizzard did. Riot also franchised *LoL* at roughly the same time as Blizzard did *Overwatch*.

However, Riot's approach to franchising was far less radical than Blizzard's at the outset. Additionally, Blizzard was first to go public with a franchising concept, announcing the OWL and its city-based structure immediately alongside *Overwatch*'s launch.[4] Furthermore, Blizzard led Riot in the franchising sales process, announcing seven franchise owners even as the LCS was just making public its application process.[5,6] For these reasons, this book credits Blizzard and the OWL with being the first to innovate esports as media properties.

Straight away, the OWL set out to cement itself as entertainment media. To do so, it copied the structure of arguably the best sports entertainment property in the world: the NFL. As such, the OWL introduced many first-time innovations to esports.

First, and most visibly, not just anyone could compete in the OWL. Activision Blizzard created a closed league, selling franchises for the then-startling price of $20 million. And unlike anything previously seen in esports before, these franchises were tied to city geographies, like Boston or Los Angeles, where the franchise owners were contractually required to establish stadia and training facilities. In fact, a significant portion of how franchise owners were expected to recoup their investment in the OWL came from local marketing and event activations. For the first time ever, esports had home teams, just like traditional sports. And in another first, these teams had uniforms—custom in-game skins and colorations—duplicating the hallowed jerseys of traditional sport.

But the OWL took things a step further still, carving out broadcast rights and global sponsorships for league-level sales, a more sophisticated approach than in previous esports. Yes, the OWL had a broadcast partner that paid handsomely for the rights to show its games online. But the OWL also secured traditional terrestrial partners—ESPN, ABC, and Disney XD— to bring the league to TVs everywhere.

Similarly, the OWL solicited much more than PC or hardware sponsors, as other leagues had in the past. Instead, the OWL debuted a sophisticated suite of multicategory sponsorships across industries as diverse as beverage (Coca-Cola), toy (Hasbro), automotive (Toyota), and more. Portions of these revenues from both broadcast and licensing, just like the NFL, were shared back with team owners to create recurring, league-driven income.

The combination of city-based teams, terrestrial media, and sponsorships suddenly made *Overwatch* much more familiar. As a result, traditional sports owners, like Robert Kraft of the New England Patriots, decided to invest in the OWL, because they realized they could now leverage their traditional sports marketing organizations to succeed in digital games. And, in a final stroke of genius, Activision Blizzard intentionally pitched and cultivated traditional sports owners as ideal OWL franchise operators. Activision Blizzard wanted the expertise and resources of franchises like the New England Patriots in play to both give credibility to their new league and to provide capital to develop it.

The initial success of the OWL, driven by its EFP approach, cannot be understated. In the first year alone, Blizzard secured millions in sponsorship and broadcast rights, in addition to the twelve teams paying $20 million each to join the league. And many of these teams were backed by traditional sports owners, with the Sacramento Kings, St. Louis Rams, and Philadelphia Flyers joining the New England Patriots to catalyze the OWL's debut.

These master strokes of tactical decision-making illustrate the A in our esports monetization BAMS model: *advertising and assets.*

Because if publishers adopted an EFP approach, they could earn money in two entirely new ways: By selling advertising, from broadcast rights to sponsorships, and by selling assets, in the form of franchises and licenses. Advertising and assets revenue brought esports out of the red. Competitive gaming was no longer a costs center draining its publishers' bank accounts. Esports were true sports. For the first time, they could make money, independent of the games that spawned them. For this reason alone, the OWL is arguably one of the most important developments in all of modern esports: it transformed esports into media.

But there is an inherent problem with the EFP and its advertising and assets approach to esports monetization, and it is a simple one: For esports to succeed as media, their underlying games must be designed to become media.

In the past, we've seen publishers succeed not just because they stumbled onto a new form of monetization, but because they integrated monetization into their game-design decisions. For example, *WoW* and *EverQuest* both pioneered subscription revenues, but *WoW* defeated its rival because it was better designed to capture subscriptions. *WoW* would not have worked had it been *Super Mario*. It succeeded because monetary innovation met design intent.

The OWL was a phenomenal, strategic decision that reshaped esports. It was the right idea, but the wrong game. *Overwatch* did not begin as an esport designed with viewership in mind. It started as the salvaged wreckage of the ambitious Titan MMO. As such, *Overwatch* lacks an essential characteristic of any sport: watchability. *Overwatch* wasn't designed to be spectator-driven. Some of these problems are solvable (a poor in-game spectating system, for example), but many are fundamental.

For example, super-heroic abilities. The same cool powers that make *Overwatch* so fun to play also make it horrendous to watch. Nowhere is this dis-complementarity more evident than in *Overwatch*'s hero character, Tracer, whose key ability is blinking, or performing short-distance teleports. This power is incredibly fun to control, but it makes Tracer's movements impossible for spectators to follow. Imagine a football match where the quarterback keeps randomly winking in and out of existence, appearing across yardage lines and end zones.

Teleportation is just one of the many mechanics in *Overwatch* designed to be played, not viewed. Overall, the superpowers in *Overwatch* offer a tangled spectator experience that leaves both new fans and experienced gamers disoriented and dissatisfied.

The OWL might have been *sold* as media, but it was not *designed* to be media.

It's important to understand that while *Overwatch* ushered in a new dawn of monetization for esports, it may not necessarily stick around to win its own game. We've seen this plenty of times before, as *EverQuest* died to *WoW* and as Atari died to Nintendo.

At the time of this writing, the jury's still out on OWL. Despite the game's early success, popularity has waned. *Overwatch* frequently falls out of the top five most watched esports.

And despite a significant increase in content hours, average viewership for the OWL has steadily declined. Average viewership for the *Overwatch* League fell below inception in 2019. And after a recent (though highly lucrative) new platform deal with YouTube for exclusivity, 2020 appears to be trending even more poorly.

However, some signs are extraordinarily positive, such as increasing grand finals viewership and an impressively expanding suite of sponsors.[7] Additionally, Blizzard announced *Overwatch* 2 in late 2019, reflecting corporate recognition of these problems, and a need to change. Nonetheless, many of the improvements planned for *Overwatch* 2, such as alternate game modes, appear to repeat old industry mistakes that bifurcate, rather than concentrate, community. It's clear *Overwatch* still has a long way to go to hold its place as a marquee esport.

But the groundbreaking innovation behind the OWL will not be lost to time. Already, the OWL has catalyzed competing publishers to introduce permanent, franchise-based models. Most significantly, Riot Games launched eight franchises for its 2018 North America League of Legends Championship Series (NA LCS), and quickly expanded thereafter. The widespread propagation of advertising and asset monetization has begun, and its reverberations continue to define esports today as more and more publishers transform their games into media.

CHAPTER EIGHT

LOOKING FOR GROUP

From the earliest days of competitive video games, teams have existed. Multiplayer battles require organized play and tight coordination. Training together as a dedicated group of gamers has just made sense, even since the early days of *Doom*.

However, the proto-teams of the '90s were little more than loosely aligned groupings of friends. These "clans" practiced and competed together, but they didn't belong to a true organization. They weren't signing contracts or receiving regular salaries.

At the turn of the millennium, as esports prizing crested into the thousands of dollars, teams began to matter more. The first year any organization is publicly recorded as earning esports prizing is 1999.[1] And almost simultaneously, the rise of *StarCraft* in Korea prompted an explosion in formalized organizations.

But the early structure of esports pro teams remained a simple quid pro quo. Gamers wanted a steady source of income to allow them to train without starving, and teams wanted a share of prizing—enough to turn a profit if the organization performed. But what began as a transactional relationship quickly evolved into one of prestige: the best players belonged to teams, so teams became a mark of both talent and authenticity. By the mid-2000s, this prestige begat sponsorships, although these remained relatively small outside of Korea.

Teams mattered a lot to pro gamers but not that much to anybody else for much of the history of esports. And while early teams might have commanded respectable pre-Twitch fandoms, they were certainly not valuable or even viable businesses. Even as late as the early 2010s, top esports teams could be bought and sold for almost nothing. For example, Jack Etienne founded Cloud9 by purchasing Quantic Gaming for about $10,000 in late 2012.[2]

So how, just six years later, did Cloud9 become the most valuable esports team in the world, with Forbes estimating their net worth at over $300 million?[3]

This massive valuation increase wasn't due entirely to the correspondingly massive increase in esports viewership, buoyed by Twitch. Even as the viewership of marquee titles like LoL spiked, team values didn't rise astronomically. As late as 2015, a top LoL team could be purchased for just $1 million,[4] and many big-name players at the time, even in the most popular games, still struggled to earn minimum wage.[5]

Instead, the introduction of the advertising and assets in the BAMS monetization model caused team valuations to explode. As publishers evolved their esports into media properties, the decision to sell franchises unintentionally gifted teams with the ultimate prize: a defensible asset.

Up until franchising, pro teams had two primary sources of revenue: prizing from taking down major tournaments and sponsorships from viewers. Both revenue streams depended on winning. The value of teams was tied purely to performance. You can't earn any money if you don't perform in tournaments, and no one wants to sponsor an organization that consistently loses. And perhaps more importantly, the most popular pro players don't want to join losing organizations.

As any traditional sports franchise owner can tell you, performance is almost impossible to guarantee. While there are rare victorious dynasties like the New York Yankees, even their perpetual dominance is mainly driven by the ownership's commitment to outspend everyone else.[6] And even the Yankees only win about one World Series every decade.

Banking on winning doesn't make for a great topline business. In fact, the Yankees' commitment to outspending the competition highlights another key problem with pre-franchise esports teams. No matter how many historical wins an organization might boast, a team is only as good as its current roster, and talent can always be purchased. As a result, team valuations in early esports were essentially capped at the sum of their contract values. Without long-term assets, the value of teams could not exceed the cost to replicate them by buying out each individual (or a comparable) pro.

So why *are* sports teams like the New York Yankees worth about $5 billion today?[7] Because they *do* have a defensible long-term asset, and that asset is a franchise. The New York Yankees own the right to participate in Major League Baseball as one of only thirty competing teams. This comes with the ability to sell sponsorships, tickets, and merchandizing in their locality. And even better: the franchise includes direct revenue sharing from MLB broadcasts, particularly of Yankee games.

As publishers like Blizzard and Riot shifted into similar media models, the OWL's and the LCS's franchising decisions created a watershed moment in the history of esports: For the first time, pro teams could own assets too.

Accordingly, in 2018 the value of pro esports teams exploded. Assuming esports is the sport of the future, teams with franchises will enjoy a permanent seat at the banquet table. As a result, in the space of just two years, over twenty top esports became worth more than $100 million. Franchising changed everything.

"It wasn't a slam-dunk decision to start my team," explains Frank Villarreal, the co-founder of Rogue, currently one of the most valuable esports organizations in the world. "But at some point, I just had to trust myself and strike out on my own."

It was November 2015. Frank was part of the (now defunct) esports team Enemy and struggling to raise capital for the fledgling organization in Las Vegas. "This was the pre-franchise era," explains Frank, "where esports viewership had begun to explode thanks to Twitch, but big venture funding hadn't yet come in. I was pounding the pavement, trying to get cash to keep Enemy afloat. At one point a friend turned to me and asked: 'Frank, why are you working this hard for someone else?'"

This simple question catalyzed Frank to consider something he hadn't before: creating his own team. He knew the esports market was primed to explode; if he was going to strike out on his own, now was the time.

"I truly struggled with the decision to leave Enemy. I worried about everyone's jobs at the organization. I thought the company would collapse if I left. So I flew back to Connecticut to meet a second-father figure to me, Lou Pressman. Lou was a philosophy professor at my old boarding school, Hotchkiss. He's someone I've turned to again and again for guidance and friendship. I needed his advice and blessing. I spent three full days with Lou over Thanksgiving, talking over my moral issues about abandoning Enemy and my fear of setting out on my own. Yeah, it was an unusual holiday."

Eventually, Lou convinced Frank that "going rogue" was the right decision, and so team Rogue was born.

"It wasn't like the team came into being overnight," Frank elaborates. "To start Rogue, we needed players. More importantly, we needed players in a particular type of game: one that was young enough to not yet be dominated by established teams, but large enough that it could generate a meaningful fanbase."

Luckily for Frank, Activision Blizzard's newest FPS *Overwatch*, was gearing up for launch. "We knew the title met all our criteria. It was a Blizzard game, so it was going to be huge. And while lots of teams were looking at *Overwatch*, none of them really had developed scouting expertise yet, or knew what to look for in pro players. There was a level playing field."

Frank still needed to pay pros to join his embryonic team, and that meant raising capital.

"I really bootstrapped it. I joined forces with my friend Sean Mulryan, and we started a consulting business called Royal Town, which is just my last name, Villarreal, translated into English. We hit the pavement in Vegas, consulting with hotel chains and random businesses trying to attract millennial audiences. That's how we survived for six months. But the whole purpose of consulting was to scout investors we liked for our esports team. As soon as we finished a contract with a good client, we pitched them our dream."

Almost immediately, Rogue faced a critical decision: "We got an offer of $250,000 for half of the company, pretty much right away. At this point we really had nothing in the bank and a quarter million was a lot of cash for esports back then. It was a super-hard decision, but we decided to believe in ourselves and turned it down."

Frank did meet one potential investor at one of these meetings, Derek Nelson, who believed enough to join as a co-founder. Now armed with a little cash, Rogue set out to aggressively hire the best talent in Overwatch.

"I already had my eye on one player: TviQ. His team, IDDQD, was breaking up, and I managed to convince him to join ours. But for the life of me I couldn't get the rest of the IDDQD squad to commit to Rogue. They had offers from a much bigger team, EnVyUs, and didn't want to risk their careers on a totally new organization. So I had one pro, but an Overwatch team requires six. We were kind of stuck."

Frank turned to James "2GD" (pronounced "Too Good") Harding, one of the founding fathers of early esports. "2GD happened to have a gamer literally living in his basement, Reinforce, who had never gone pro in his life. Somehow 2GD discovered he was an amazing Tank in Overwatch. By convincing Reinforce to pair up with TviQ, we now had the core of a squad. With excellent Tank and DPS [damage per second] players, we could start convincing other pros to join."

But capital still remained a constraint. Having turned down that quarter-million-dollar check, Rogue didn't have much money after hiring TviQ and Reinforce.

"We turned to France," explains Frank. "We knew some French players who were really good, and the market there was undervalued because of the language barrier. In the early stages of Rogue, we didn't care about marketing or sponsorships, we just cared about winning. 2GD suggested we pick up the best French pros we could and we didn't really have much of a choice. Our final squad ended up being a bit of a mishmash: three French pros and three Swedes. There was a lot of culture clashing, but in terms of ability, the team was top rate."

Armed with a full roster at last, Rogue set out to make a name for itself.

"We knew the bar for success was incredibly high. If we weren't winning big in the first six months of the organization, we were dead. It was literally do or die time for Rogue. No one funds a losing esports team for very long."

Frank's international talent scouting paid off. "Almost immediately we started winning. We took down the very first *Overwatch* tournament, an online cup on launch day. Immediately after that we won the first European LAN. But there was a perception amongst gamers that Europe didn't matter, because the best pros played in America, despite there being no evidence of this fact. So Rogue came to the first Unified Major, the Atlantic Showdown, with something to prove. This was the first-ever *Overwatch* event to feature major teams from both Europe and America and we knew we had to win."

Frank explains, "The semifinals of that event were legendary. We were matched against EnVyUs, our old nemesis who'd snatched those IDDQD pros, and the best North American organization. To this day, many people consider this series the greatest *Overwatch* match of all time. We fought to the very end of the seven-game series, four to three, with every game going the distance. After winning the semifinals, we knew we had the whole tournament on lock."

Frank's victory couldn't have come at a better time. Because by a fluke of fate, Steve Aoki, the electronic dance music (EDM) icon, was about to learn of Rogue's success.

Frank continues, "My co-founder's brother, Joel Nelson, used to work at a money management firm with Matt Colon, who is Steve Aoki's manager. Just by chance, Matt called Joel to complain about Steve wanting to start his own esports team.

'I don't know how Steve thinks he has the time to run his own team. This is just going to end up being a ton of work for me,' he said, and Joel told him, 'My brother just started an esports team, and they're pretty good....'"

The team immediately pitched Steve Aoki on investing in the business because they recognized his strategic value. Beyond capital, Steve presented a hook for future investors. With a celebrity on board, Rogue would feel like a safer investment. And of course, as a Vegas icon, Steve would help build early traction and fans for the team.

"The actual signing with Steve happened during the Atlanta ELEAGUE tournament," Frank recalls. "Derek and I watched our matches from the bleachers, then Matt or Steve would ring us and we'd run to the greenroom and work on the deal. We were actually at a tournament as the deal was signed. That Saturday night we took the Rogue pros to Benihana's—which is actually owned by the Aoki family—as a tribute to Steve and told them the good news. Immediately afterwards, Derek and I booked flights to TwitchCon [a major gaming event hosted by Twitch], where Steve was going to perform."

Frank beams as he recalls his moment of triumph. "The next morning we were on a plane. We literally wrote the press release in some random café in San Diego then headed straight backstage at the Padres stadium to meet Steve. So there we were in these dark passages, with Steve jamming on stage in front of a huge TwitchCon crowd. And Eliza, Steve's tour manager, comes over to us with a full bottle of whiskey. And she says, 'You guys look nervous, drink up. Because Steve wants you to go on stage too.' So Sean and I were shooting straight out of a bottle, trying to calm our nerves. It was a surreal moment of culmination. Then we went on stage with Steve and in front of the entire Twitch community, he announced his investment in Rogue.

That was obviously the turning point for our organization."

Except it wasn't, because a massive disaster loomed around the corner.

As good as franchising can be for some teams, it can be devastating for others. And because of franchising, Rogue was about to face the biggest challenge of its short life.

"When we heard the Overwatch League was going to sell permanent slots we were extremely excited. We knew right away how important this was. We *had* to get a place in the league. It wouldn't matter how big or successful our team might become. Without the rights to compete in *Overwatch*, our followers would disappear and our early traction would mean nothing. Franchising was the start of the process of institutional money coming into esports, and that money was going to decide the winners and losers of modern gaming. Owning an *Overwatch* franchise was all that mattered. It would secure Rogue's place in the next phase of growth in our industry."

Frank and the Rogue team set out to raise the $20 million required to purchase a permanent home for their team. Buoyed by Steve Aoki's reputation, they quickly synced up with ReKTGlobal, a top esports development consultancy, which offered to source the full financing round. Amazingly, less than a month and a half later, ReKT came through.

Frank remembers, "I felt like it was all coming together. We had a winning team. A big celebrity investor. Millions in funding lined up. How could we *not* succeed?"

Here's how: Rogue was denied a franchise slot in the OWL.

"Failing to franchise almost destroyed the business," Frank recalls. "It was a category-ten disaster. It meant everything we had built in *Overwatch* was worth nothing, overnight.

"I literally spent twenty-four hours floating in a pool," Frank explains. "I didn't know what else to do. Everyone was crushed: the pros, my friends, Steve Aoki. It was like the entire organization was grieving. It was like a death. A lights-out moment."

Franchises are valuable precisely because of what they exclude. And the pain of this exclusion is what Rogue, and dozens of other upstart and mainstream *Overwatch* teams, learned the hard way.

"We were dead in *Overwatch*," Frank says. "Blizzard's single decision destroyed our entire business model. Being on the outside of a franchise game is not a viable business. It relegates your organization, at best, to a farm team. So we let go every single one of our *Overwatch* pros almost immediately. All of our success in that game was wiped away."

But that didn't mean Rogue was wiped away. As Frank took stock of the situation, he saw a path forward. "We realized we still had all the ingredients: Top management. A big celebrity. And with ReKT, we had capital and network, too. In the end, it was someone else's decision that held Rogue back. So I decided to double down with ReKT and go after another franchise."

A deal emerged: Rogue would become a subsidiary of ReKT, who would in turn purchase a substantial share of Rogue. "We looked at Frank's business," explains Kevin Knocke, chief creative officer of ReKTGlobal, "and particularly liked how Rogue was aligned with entertainment and Steve Aoki. We saw teams more and more as being marketed as entertainment so even without *Overwatch*, we thought we could still build something special. We did the deal."

Together, Rogue and ReKT set out to hunt the only other franchised esports at the time: *League of Legends*. "We'd missed the North American slots," explains Frank, "so we went as hard as we could at buying a slot in the European League. I wish I could say this was another crazy story, but it wasn't. The second time proved the charm. With a lot of hard work, and careful planning, our pitch paid off and Rogue entered the big leagues."

Today Rogue is one of the largest and most successful pro teams in the world. "I had an amazing moment when I went back to tell Professor Lou what had happened," Frank says. "He told me he was retiring from teaching, and that the story of my success was the perfect capstone to his educational career."

But Rogue's tale is more than just the story of one organization's rise to prominence. It is a clear indication of the risks and benefits of franchising—and how this trend is reshaping the entire esports industry.

"Franchising will continue to happen in every major game," explains Frank. "It is the inevitable next step in esports. Everyone you speak to, in every other major organization, will agree. Franchising is the future of esports."

But is this a good thing?

"Absolutely," says Frank. "Franchising is a stabilizing force for the industry. Teams are defensible now because they are guaranteed an audience in their game. And franchises come with revenue streams from league-level sponsorships and broadcast rights. These payments bring security: if the game as a whole is healthy, its franchises will be viable, even if individual teams underperform."

Kevin of ReKT adds, "There's another reason franchises matter. A lot of people think the high price tags on franchises go to waste. Like the teams are throwing away twenty or thirty million dollars. But this is simply not true. That money is going into an asset, with a monetary value associated with it. Buying franchises is just like buying real estate. You're making a long-term investment in a marketable commodity. And just like real-estate investments, not all league investments are created equal. Some are better targets for short-term growth, some for long-term sustainability. You need to know the underlying trends driving the franchise you are buying, but you are still buying a real asset."

"And then there's power," Frank adds. "The publishers have the vast majority of the power in our industry now. You saw that with how Rogue was almost destroyed by one decision from Activision Blizzard. But franchises are a way for teams to take back control. They are the publishers giving away rights permanently. And because of the high price tags, franchises also bring heavyweight institutional investors to the table, people like the Krafts [owner of the New England Patriots] and the Wilpons [majority owner of the New York Mets], who can and *do* effectively push back against the publishers. The industry dynamic is shifting. More and more, maybe without even realizing it, the publishers are creating market conditions that limit their own strength. The publishers will always be a powerful force in our industry," Frank concludes. "But right now, the teams are rising in power, too."

CHAPTER NINE

GO FOR PRO

William "Amnesiac" Barton got into video games for a classic reason: sibling rivalry. "I started playing on consoles with my brother, Gene. We were four years apart, so video games became an easy way to bridge an awkward age gap. It was something we could do together."

At first Barton played casually, but soon he discovered competitive gaming just as it was taking off. "When Gene got into *StarCraft II*, I was ten, so I couldn't really play it myself," he explains. "My parents hadn't even bought me my own computer yet. So I watched my brother play. A lot. It became an easy jump for me to watch *other* people play. I became a fan of the scene, following different gamers online."

Barton's story is typical of the emerging generation of pro gamers. Just as amateur athletes are inspired by observing professionals, Barton became fascinated by gamers who were good at *StarCraft*. "I wouldn't say idolize. It's more like, I watched what they were doing and thought, I can do that too. I can be just as good."

Barton's life changed when his favorite streamer, Sean "Day9" Plott, tried out the closed beta test of a new CCG: *Hearthstone*.

Barton soon downloaded the game, too. "I was naturally good at it. I got Legend [the highest rank] in two weeks."

WHAT ARE CCGS?

We've talked about esports in the FPS, RTS, and MOBA genres. Collectible card games (CCGs; sometimes referred to as trading card games or digital card games), are a fourth major genre of esports, and emphasize strategy over reflexes.

In CCGs, players assemble a deck of virtual cards from an expansive library of options. Each card has unique powers and abilities, as well as a specific cost to play or activate. Players then take turns placing their cards onto a virtual landscape or board, attempting to overwhelm their opponent with quick combinations of abilities, or by delaying the game until more powerful, but higher-cost, cards can be activated. CCGs are often given a fantasy flavor, with cards depicting Tolkien-esque creatures and heroic spells.

All CCGs are strongly inspired by (and some might even say directly copy) paper card games like Magic: The Gathering. In fact, Magic itself has recently joined the esports landscape with its own digital product, *Magic: Arena*.

In the space of just fourteen days, fourteen-year-old Barton had done the seemingly impossible: transition from watching *Hearthstone* to numbering in the top 0.1 percent of its millions of players. Obviously, Barton is naturally talented; but even so, how was such a meteoric rise possible?

"For esports, watching can be really good practice," he explains. "I think it's part of why Twitch is so popular. I studied how the pros played *Hearthstone* before I ever downloaded it. And I used that time to pick up all the fundamentals: not just game mechanics, but strategy. I firmly believe anyone can do the same. Esports are incredibly accessible if you approach them like a student, trying to learn."

But hitting Legend had another unique aspect that proved deeply motivating for Barton: a leaderboard.

"For the first time, I could look at a number by my username and see exactly how good I was: Legend Number 117," he says. "I was almost in the hundred best players in the world. I'd never thought of myself as being a pro gamer. I knew I was above average at games, but now it was clear to me exactly how good I was."

In this regard, esports are unique. It's not possible for a high school quarterback to know with machine precision exactly how good at football he is. But in esports, thanks to the constantly updating ranking systems used for match pairings, it's effortless to know your exact level of proficiency. This visibility also makes the path to pro much more attainable. Not only can you play esports in the comfort of your own home, but you can see exactly how you are improving, day by day, how far you've come, and how far you still have to go.

"It can be addicting," explains Barton. "In a good way."

It's important to interject that despite Barton being a talented gamer, he is by no means the clichéd image of a basement-dwelling nerd. In fact, most modern pro gamers are nothing like the stereotype. "I was very healthy growing up," he explains. "I played soccer, basketball, and football." (Barton is also an extremely accomplished tennis player.) "I guess I'm a competitive person, and I just saw games as another avenue to be competitive. Gaming—even professional gaming—can be part of a balanced lifestyle."

In fact, Barton's well-rounded nature was part of what let his parents feel comfortable with him devoting himself to *Hearthstone*.

"There I was in eighth grade, doing well in school and playing sports. And I still found I had downtime, about four hours a day. I thought to myself: okay, let's give this *Hearthstone* thing a shot. Let's see how good I can get."

Around this time, another pro gamer, Jason "Amaz" Chan, began to develop a friendship with Barton through their in-game interactions. Chan belonged to the first generation of pro gamers who supported themselves almost entirely from Twitch income. Given how good Barton was, Chan began encouraging him to start streaming as well.

"Amaz helped me set up," Barton explains. "Got everything going. And then I could just play like I had already been doing. Except now I was broadcasting at the same time, to a live audience. Three or four hours a day, every day. And just like that, after about two months, I had over one thousand viewers."

Again, the accessibility of esports comes into focus. The barrier to becoming a celebrity in traditional sports is huge. But because of the digital nature of esports, it was a simple step for Barton to go from playing *Hearthstone* to broadcasting *Hearthstone*; in esports the two are often synonymous.

But hosting a successful Twitch channel had another benefit: it turned a hobby into a job. "I could make money gaming," Barton explains. "There was a financial return to my time. It was like a part-time job *and* a video game in one."

Barton redoubled his commitment to *Hearthstone*, leading Chan to offer him a coveted slot on Team Archon. Part of the appeal of Chan's offer was that he could help grow Barton's income, both by supporting his stream and through a direct salary as a pro gamer.

"I enlisted my brother Gene to explain to my mom and dad that I wasn't going to be murdered or scammed," continued Barton. "I think they had a hard time believing a high school freshman could go pro at anything. But my parents are awesome, and seeing the money I was starting to make, I think they understood there was something legitimate here. So I joined Archon that same week and started playing in tournaments."

But this first step into the proverbial spotlight proved challenging. In some sense, it was the first wakeup call to Barton as to how far he had come.

"My first-ever esports event was the *Hearthstone* regional qualifiers in September 2015. I was super nervous," he explains. "I couldn't eat the day I played. That's something I never really had to deal with before: nerves. I ended up not doing so well, but it didn't matter. It was my first tournament. I realized that things were going to be different. That this wasn't just a hobby, but a real profession. And an amazing opportunity. I knew that if I worked hard, I would do better in the next event."

Almost prophetically, Barton's breakout success came immediately after.

"I won the next qualifier. I remember my dad took me. Because I was so young I had to have a legal guardian present. And then after that I won the Winter Championships with my mom watching. I think that really brought home to both my parents what it was to be a pro gamer, and the success I was experiencing."

Barton's rise to become one of the best *Hearthstone* players, with his first championship title, occurred blisteringly fast. But his success also further highlights the accessibility of modern esports. It would literally be impossible, for example, for a fourteen-year-old to go directly into the NBA. But esports' egalitarian nature ensured that Barton's success was only limited by his talent.

Unfortunately, Barton did not win the 2016 Hearthstone World Championships. But he did make the top eight, taking home an impressive $50,000. More importantly, "Young Savage," as he was affectionately called by his fans, cemented a reputation: he was the youngest pro ever to qualify for the Hearthstone World Championships. Barton numbered among the most distinguished gamers in one of esports' most popular titles, all while still a freshman in high school.

THE LEGEND OF AMNESIAC

Most pro gamers have an unusual, or apocryphal, story about how they choose their gamer name. It's a point of pride—or embarrassment. William Barton's story is no different.

"I compete under the name Amnesiac. And I chose it because I thought pro gamers need to have a cool, one-word name. At the time, I was into *StarCraft*, and my brother was playing *Amnesia: The Dark Descent*, so I merged them together, into Amnesia_StarCraft, and then just AmnesiaSC. In *Hearthstone*, people kept misreading it as 'Amnesiac' and I was like, 'Yeah, that's way cooler.' So that's how I got my gamer name."

"It was hard to focus on class after that," Barton admits. "Around this time my parents *did* start to get mad at me. Like, 'You need to try harder in history.' That sort of thing. But it's a question of priorities, and it was hard to prioritize school when it was so clear where I was most rewarded. I don't think this is a problem with esports. It's just something that happens to people who have success when they're young. It would be the same with a talented teenage golfer or cellist."

Barton's reputation began to draw the attention of larger pro teams.

"I remember getting signed to NRG [pro team NRG Esports] in 2017. It was the first time I had free agency, and Andy Miller recruited me. That was wild. I looked at Andy's background—a very successful Silicon Valley entrepreneur, owner of the

Sacramento Kings—and I was blown away. I couldn't believe this guy wanted me on his team. I knew Shaquille O'Neal was involved with NRG, too, so telling people I was going to be gaming with Shaq was pretty awesome."

But it wasn't just esports organizations that wanted a piece of Barton. "Redbull called almost immediately afterward. Now *that* was surreal. I remember meeting their exec with my dad—my guardian still had to be there—and we both could feel the interview going well. Driving home my dad looked at me and said, 'They are going to pick you up.' And he was right: I was sponsored by Redbull a few weeks after that. The youngest-ever Redbull gamer."

Obviously, this meant significant financial success for Amnesiac, who was still in his first year of high school. But the height of Barton's rise still didn't really sink in until around the holidays that year.

"Everything came into perspective at Christmas. I'm pretty hard to buy gifts for, you know, since I make a lot of money gaming. And I knew my family was planning something special. But I couldn't think what it would be. Well, on Christmas morning I found that my sister had built me a trophy case for everything I'd won. My parents had even framed my esports jersey. That was pretty unbelievable. I could look at my tangible accomplishments, and also see they meant something to my family. That they were also proud of what I had done."

So what advice would Barton have to other aspiring gamers who might want to follow in his footsteps?

"Streaming is the most important part of becoming a pro gamer," he says. "That's my main piece of advice to aspiring pros: start streaming. No one will care about you if you don't stream. In today's market, to become a popular streamer you have to differentiate yourself. The question you need to ask is: Why is your stream better than Ninja's? Or mine? You need uniqueness. And skill often—not always—is not enough. You are also an entertainer. My point of difference was my age. I was the Young Savage! But you need to find what makes you special. If you don't have it, you won't get to the top."

But the path to success as a pro gamer also comes with a warning.

"You might like playing video games, but that doesn't necessarily mean you'll like being a pro gamer," he says. "I discovered going pro is a profession. A job. A lot of people play games to escape real life. But it's the opposite as a pro. Gaming *becomes* your real life. There is no escape anymore."

Today, William "Amnesiac" Barton has won over $150,000 playing *Hearthstone*, but his career income approaches seven figures with his numerous sponsorships, particularly Redbull. And, most importantly—and perhaps unsurprisingly—gaming helped him get into college. At the time of this writing, he's stepped away from pro gaming to focus on his classes at Northwestern. Parents, take notice: "My background was an asset in the college admissions process," Barton advises. "It's a notable skill, just like being a talented trombonist or student athlete."

The important takeaway from Barton's story is not the meteoric heights of his success, but how effortlessly he was able to achieve it. Thanks to the accessibility of modern esports, his journey to stardom was uniquely possible.

This, more than anything else, is the appeal of esports. We can all see ourselves in each and every pro gamer. We imagine ourselves like them. And we can clearly see the rungs in the ladder of imitation and idolization. Download the game. Play a ranked season. Start streaming. Every step toward stardom leads naturally to the next.

As we learn from Amnesiac, esports are not about retreating into a digital world, but embracing a human skill. "That's the most important thing for people to take away from my story," Barton concludes. "Pro gaming can be balanced. I still went to the gym. I still had friends. Esports helped me get into college and I'm doing well. Pro gaming isn't the end of normal life. It's an opportunity to live life more fully."

CHAPTER TEN

KETCHUP OR MUSTARD?

W e've seen how popular games like *Hearthstone*, *League of Legends*, and *Overwatch* have defined the landscape of modern esports. But uncertainty clouds the future of every one of these titles. Are they here to stay, like traditional sports? Or are they fated to perpetually cycle, like traditional video games?

This is the "ketchup or mustard" question. Because these two condiments neatly illustrate how two things that appear very similar on the surface—esports and sports, ketchup and mustard—can produced vastly different consumer markets.

Let's start with ketchup. Depending on the continent you are on, Heinz dominates the market. And even the brands that aren't Heinz, like store brands, are made to *taste* like Heinz. Sure, there are fancy flavors, like sweet maple and Sriracha, but these represent a tiny portion of all ketchup sales. When it comes to ketchup, we know what we like. We want ketchup to taste a certain way.

But across the aisle from the ketchups are the mustards. There isn't one dominant flavor of mustard. Instead there's a world of diversity: spicy, honey, whole grain, and more. And we want all these different types of mustard on different occasions.

You might prefer classic yellow on a hot dog, but Dijon on a burger. Unlike ketchup, we can't agree on what mustard should taste like. We crave variety.

Traditional sports, like football and soccer, are ketchups. There might be many permutations of stick-and-ball sports, for example, but major regions have settled around their preferred game. Cricket isn't going anywhere in India. Baseball is firmly entrenched in the US. And the historical trend has been toward convergence. Even though there were differing regional rules, baseball eventually consolidated into the American and National Leagues (and in turn, Major League Baseball).

In contrast to sports, video games are mustards. Even within genre, there are hundreds of new titles every year. No one agrees which is the best, because games are subjective experiences. And variety and novelty matter greatly, so every month consumers stop playing their old titles to enjoy the next major release.

The answer to the question "Are esports ketchup or mustard?" determines how successful esports as a whole will become. If esports are like sports (ketchup) then this permanence permits long-term value. Ketchup justifies building huge stadiums and spending billions for pro teams. As an athlete, it means you can train your whole life in a single game, confident that when you are ready, your esport of choice will still be there. And crucially, ketchup creates intergenerational experiences. Will you be watching *Overwatch* matches with your grandson, just like your grandfather watched baseball with you?

Sports are worth big money because they are here to stay.

In contrast, the mustard paradigm of esports is lawless and terrifying. No one title will achieve dominance, and a vast variety of games will come and go. Consumers will always enjoy watching and playing esports—that much is certain—but *what* we watch and play may change too rapidly for the industry to stabilize. Everything being built today will be wasted. Teams, leagues, and even sponsorships won't make sense because games won't last long enough to justify investment.

So which are esports, ketchup or mustard? To answer this question, we need to tell the story of the most successful esport of all.

Battle Royale is a classic Japanese film from 2000 that tells the dystopian story of high schoolers randomly selected for imprisonment. After being provided with minimal equipment, the students must fend for themselves in a *Lord of the Flies* scenario. There's just one catch: The high schoolers must murder each other to survive.

Battle Royale proved a massive hit in Asia, and an outsized cultural influence globally. Western hits like *The Hunger Games* borrow many elements from the film (although author Suzanne Collins maintains she had never heard of *Battle Royale* when she began writing).[1]

The surging popularity of these stories created the term "battle royale" and a desire to play out similar, one-versus-everyone storylines in modern gaming.

The most significant early effort was a mod for 2009's *ARMA 2*. In *DayZ*, players scavenge equipment and massacre zombies, all while murdering other players for better gear and a stronger chance at survival.

DayZ garnered about a million users at the time of the mod's standalone launch in 2013. But in simulating its zombie-scavenger fantasy, *DayZ* also created a strangely barren

WHAT'S A BATTLE ROYALE?

Battle royales (BRs) are another major genre of esports. Superficially, they are similar to FPS games like *Overwatch* in that you control a single hero who attempts to eliminate other players using various guns and special abilities.

However, while FPSs focus on tight team-based combat, BRs embrace the intensity and chaos of few-versus-many massacres. BRs also generally feature a shrinking play area to force gamers to keep fighting as the death toll rises. And BRs aren't always played from a first-person perspective. For example, the popular BR *Fortnite* controls from an over-the-shoulder viewpoint.

world. The game eschewed centralized battle points, instead encouraging solitary exploration for randomly dispersed supplies.

And then came Brendan Greene, going by the alias "PlayerUnknown." Brendan bounced between freelance photography and unemployment, but in his digital life, he sought to refine *DayZ* into a more visceral experience. Directly influenced by the Japanese film, Brendan released *DayZ: Battle Royale*. The mod proved popular, jumpstarting Brendan's game development career. So in 2015, Brendan found himself on a plane to South Korea to meet with a relatively unknown developer, Bluehole, to discuss the possibility of helming a wholly original BR title. And while no one had guessed it at the time, a dangerous revolution in esports had begun.

After a blisteringly fast development timeline, *PlayerUnknown's Battlegrounds* (PUBG) launched to early access (essentially a commercialized pre-release) in March 2017. A clear development vision, heavy usage of open market assets, and a liberal amount of corner-cutting (resulting in a buggy game), allowed *PUBG* to lightning-sprint to market.

In *PUBG*, you join a 100-person free-for-all by jumping out of an airplane. You land in an abandoned wilderness city, scavenge what you can, and kill to survive in search of the elusive "Chicken Dinner"—*PUBG*'s term for last man standing. This frenetic gameplay created an overnight success.

PUBG made $11 million in its first three days, paying for the entirety of its development.[2] Three weeks later, *PUBG* neared 100,000 simultaneous users; just four months later, it crossed the $100 million revenue mark with over 6 million units sold.[3] Just as excitement geared up for the Overwatch League, an obscure game from an unknown Korean publisher suddenly outperformed Blizzard's marquee shooter. The BR genre was born.

But why did *PUBG* triumph where *DayZ* had failed? Because Brendan eliminated the barrenness plaguing prior BRs. *PUBG* perfected a gameplay mechanic called the Exclusion Zone: an ever-shrinking circle of "permissible terrain" outside of which players were damaged and killed. While past BRs had employed similar concepts, *PUBG* was the first to nail its implementation. As a result, *PUBG*'s Zone forced players into constant contact, relentlessly generating dynamic and tension-filled moments of ambush and assault. And as more players died, the Zone shrank to intensify the conflict and to ratchet up the pace of the game.

But the Exclusion Zone didn't just make *PUBG* more fun. Crucially, it improved a SCAR factor by making BRs more skill-intensive. In previous BRs, it was possible to win simply by concealing yourself in an obscure corner of the map, until everyone had killed each other off. But because of *PUBG*'s

Exclusion Zone, stealth became much less effective. Run-and-gun reflexes now mattered more than the patience to outwait the competition.

PUBG also improved another SCAR factor: accessibility. Because of the chaotic size of 100-person free-for-alls, strict matchmaking wasn't required. As a result, almost the instant players queued up in *PUBG*, they airdropped into a new match without the two- to five-minute wait times that bogged down traditional FPS games due to complicated matchmaking algorithms. Even better, as soon as a gamer died in *PUBG*, they weren't stuck waiting for the match to complete as in a traditional team-based FPS. They could instantly requeue: getting right back on a new plane to parachute into a new battlefield.

By improving skill and accessibility, *PUBG* grew into a gaming juggernaut, grossing nearly $1 billion with 30 million copies sold.[4] Console releases brought the PC experience to more fans, particularly when *PUBG* became packaged with new Xbox One purchases. And just three months later, in March 2018, 87 million players logged in on a single day to experience *PUBG*'s frenetic action.[5] An incredibly fun and polished version of *PUBG* even debuted on mobile, garnering over 100 million downloads by August of that year.

By every single metric, *PUBG* was a massive success. So how was it possible that just a few months later, the most popular game in esports' hottest new genre entered a death spiral?

Fortnite began development in 2011 as a team-based zombie-defense game, with squads of four players erecting protective structures against an AI-controlled horde. This focus on human versus machine proved lackluster. And *Fortnite* suffered from a six-year development cycle, delayed because of a switch to the newest version of its publisher Epic's proprietary Unreal 4 engine. As a result, *Fortnite* flopped when it launched six years later to early access. Nobody cared. It was just another zombie hunt.

Except that *Fortnite*'s team noticed the success of *PUBG* and fell in love with the game. In turn, Epic rapidly accelerated development of *Fortnite: Battle Royale*, an almost direct copy of *PUBG* in the *Fortnite* game client. The team somehow managed to finish this entire overhaul—shifting the focus of *Fortnite* from base defense to hundred-player chaos—in the space of a few months.

When *Fortnite: Battle Royale* launched in September 2017, gamers paid attention because it relaunched as free-to-play.[6] Epic understood that to catch *PUBG*, they needed to grow their player base as rapidly as possible, so they copied the pricing strategy *League of Legends* used to dethrone *Heroes of Newerth*. *PUBG*'s $29.99 price was a handbrake on its success compared to *Fortnite*'s free-for-everyone approach.

As a result, *Fortnite: Battle Royale* blasted to 10 million users within two weeks of launch.[7] Barely a year later, *Fortnite: Battle Royale* was truncated to just *Fortnite* and grossed $2.4 billion annually, across 125 million users and climbing, resulting in a capital raise by Epic Games of over $1 billion to cement its dominance.[8]

But while monetization was the most important factor leading to its success, *Fortnite* did four other things right to dethrone *PUBG*.

First, *Fortnite* wasn't more accessible just because it was free. The game also featured a cartoonish and comedic art style, making it appeal to a wider audience than *PUBG*'s gritty military aesthetic.

Second, *Fortnite* continued to raise the skill of BRs with its elaborately comical building mechanic. This feature was originally part of *Fortnite* to allow gamers to quickly protect themselves from zombies, but when repurposed into BR conflicts, the ability to create defenses on the fly dialed up the skill required to win. Now it was possible to control the environment around the player, minimizing the danger of ambushes and outright random deaths thanks to instantaneous cover and immediate tactical advantage.

Thirdly, *Fortnite* committed to one of the most aggressive new content schedules in the history of gaming. At first updates launched monthly, then weekly. The fresh stream of items and abilities amplified the BR genre's gleeful chaos—there was almost always something new to discover, something different to experiment with.

And this rapid content drip was buoyed by a final smart decision from Epic Games (again copying from Riot's playbook) to not release another map, but rather to constantly evolve the same location with everchanging story events. The result was a game that was always different enough to be fun, but familiar enough to be welcoming. And while the constant content updates led to questions about grueling working conditions at Epic, it was clear that the approach worked in market.[9]

Fortnite crushed *PUBG*.

To be fair, *PUBG* was also partly responsible for its own downfall. The lingering bugs from rushed development came home to roost, resulting in the infamous "Fix *PUBG*" campaign started by Bluehole itself. Rather than streaming out new content to compete with *Fortnite*'s evolution, *PUBG* was stuck spending resources to repair its core game. This problem was amplified by *PUBG*'s decision to devote resources to new maps: a strategic mistake that only bifurcated its player base.

Fortnite deserved to win.

But what does this tell us about ketchup and mustard? *Fortnite* might be the best BR today, but does that prevent another BR from dethroning it next year? Just like *Fortnite* itself dethroned *PUBG*?[10]

In early 2019, *Apex Legends* launched out of nowhere to challenge *Fortnite* for the BR crown. *Apex* employed an entirely novel marketing strategy of total blackout, then media barrage. Three weeks before its launch, no one had heard of *Apex*. There had been no previews, nor pre-media campaign, nor tradeshow demos. This wasn't laziness on developer Respawn's part: it was incredibly effective planning. Building for one massive, concentrated surprise.

Most gamers learned of *Apex* on its launch day. At the same exact moment, nearly every single major *Fortnite* streamer was paid to switch over to *Apex* for an entire week, driving millions of gamers to Google the title and discover that *Apex* was in fact a real game, and that it was now publicly available.

And it was free to play.

As a result, *Apex* blew past almost every major milestone of video game growth. Within twenty-four hours, over 2 million were battling it out on *Apex*'s servers. At one week, 25 million. At one month, 50 million. *Apex* broke monetization records, too, becoming the highest-earning F2P game ever during its launch month.[11]

When *Apex* had first dropped, the vice president of Epic Games, Mark Rein, must have felt invincible, tweeting his congratulations to *Apex* developer Respawn Entertainment and encouraging gamers to check it out. The tweet was promptly deleted. Just days later, *Fortnite* went into damage-control mode to combat the sudden juggernaut: even buying *Fortnite* ads keyed to search terms like "Apex Legends" on Google.

But *Apex Legends* was ultimately not able to dethrone *Fortnite*. Despite its incredible early traction, just a few short months later the title found itself in decline, and *Fortnite* finished 2019 as the highest-growing video game of the year, earning over $1.8 billion.[12] While this was a terrible result for Respawn, it was a fantastic outcome for esports.

Fortnite's continued dominance of the BR genre suggests that esports can be ketchups. Just like early baseball, there might be churn in the early days as genres find their footing. But ultimately, the trend is toward stability.

But why did *Fortnite* endure? What, exactly, makes it ketchup?

The final framework of this book, OMENS, predicts how stable an esports title is. Essentially, if it is ketchup or mustard. The **OMENS** framework also combines many of the concepts we've seen earlier in this book into its five defensibility factors:

Opportunities for competition – How large and successful is the game currently? Is it its market leader, or a new entrant? How many similar titles currently exist in market, and how easy is it for another publisher to create a similar game?

Monetization – How sophisticated is the BAMS monetization model employed by the game? How aggressively does the game reinvest its profits into future development? Could lower-quality games gain traction by being cheaper?

Ecosystem support – How rewarding is the competitive ecosystem built around the game? How tethered are celebrities and teams to the title? How important is community-generated content to promoting and mastering the game?

Network effects – How important is a large number of users in matchmaking and in-game market-making? How much social interaction does the game facilitate, and how does the game encourage virality amongst users?

Switching costs – How important is a collection of digital assets to gameplay, and how difficult are they to acquire? How unique are the skills required to get good at the game, and how quickly does a new player develop these skills?

OMENS explains why *PUBG* failed to hold its ground against *Fortnite*, while *Fortnite* weathered the storm brought on by *Apex*.

PUBG fails almost every single one of the OMENS tests. *PUBG* was made quickly, largely with off-the-shelf assets, easily allowing a competitor with even a limited timeline and resources to duplicate what had been built (O). *PUBG* also employed a traditional blades monetization model, allowing competition on price, and could not reinvest resources in new content because it still had to repair a buggy game (M). And as *PUBG* built toward success, it did nothing to create a competitive ecosystem around its game to lock in devoted players (E). Worse, *PUBG*'s non-skilled matchmaking meant that large numbers of users were not important to market liquidity—any game that could have 100 players in queue at once could compete (N). And the skills required to play *PUBG* were generic military shooter skills, without much specialized talent required to excel (S).

As a result, *PUBG* was destined to be dethroned.

It's important to clarify, though, that OMENS *does not* predict a title's initial success. *PUBG*, after all, was a huge hit at launch. Rather, OMENS determines whether or not a title can maintain its success indefinitely. If the title is a traditional video game (mustard), or a true esport (ketchup).

Now let's apply the OMENS framework to *Fortnite*.

Fortnite: Battle Royale might have been rushed out, but

the underlying game had been in development for six years, using a wholly owned engine (O). *Fortnite* launched as free-to-play, and aggressively reinvested earnings into new content (M). *Fortnite* actively promoted community investment in the game, including launching one of the highest-prized esports championships in the world (E). And *Fortnite* eventually introduced skill-based matchmaking, to take advantage of its ballooning player base (N). Finally, *Fortnite*'s building mechanic required unique skills to master, not easily transferable to other games (S).

Fortnite's continued success highlights another nuance of OMENS: titles don't need to launch with every factor to endure. Modern games evolve over their lifetime. Smart developers can improve their OMENS post-launch, entrenching a successful game like building a moat around a castle.

OMENS has one final crucial implication: Not every title claiming to be an esport today—even a successful one—is *actually* an esport. Using OMENS, we can evaluate these games for permanency.

OMENS speaks to the true potential of esports. Fears of a mustard universe are unfounded. While many esports titles today may not survive, many others should. And even those games badly positioned for longevity today can evolve into enduring brands.

READING THE OMENS

Let's use our OMENS framework to evaluate the two biggest esports previously discussed in this book: *Overwatch* and *League of Legends*. Are these games destined to stick around?

Let's start with *LoL*. This title is rock-solid (something you might have already guessed, given that it already fended off both *Dota 2* and *Heroes of the Storm*). While *LoL*'s five-on-five heroic brawls are easy to replicate in principle, its incredibly balanced gameplay is a nightmare to clone (O). *LoL* is free-to-play (M), and has invested in one of the largest and most sophisticated competitive ecosystems in the world (E). *LoL* also benefits enormously from community resources to navigate its obtuse mechanics, in addition to relying extensively on skill-based matchmaking that requires assembling balanced groupings of champions (N). Finally, *LoL* encourages its users to assemble a large collection of heroes, each with unique skills to master (S).

Overwatch is much more of a mixed bag. It uses a blades business model, easily allowing competitors to undercut its price. And the game is also slow to reinvest profits in meaningful updates. For example, *Overwatch* has only added nine new heroes since launch (M). Its streamlined gameplay benefits less from elaborate guides, and its matchmaking doesn't require as much liquidity as *LoL*'s (E). Worst of all, *Overwatch* requires largely generic aim-and-shoot skills, and doesn't encourage collecting a library of unique heroes (S).

But *Overwatch* also has an elaborate and extensively promoted esports scene (N). Will this be enough to keep this game around?

The answer lies in our O factor. In February of 2019, Activision Blizzard announced the *Call of Duty (CoD) World League*. *Call of Duty* is owned by Activision Blizzard, just like *Overwatch*. *CoD* is an FPS, just like *Overwatch*. It is franchised, just like *Overwatch*. And if you bought a team in Activision Blizzard's original league, you aren't included in *CoD*. In one fell swoop, Activision Blizzard created its own competitor!

Consider the NFL. Suppose its commissioner created the IFL, or International Football League, with a completely new set of teams. Imagine having IFL franchises set up shop in every US city, directly competing for

NFL teams' market share, yet still fully sanctioned by the NFL. As a fan, who would you root for now that you have two home teams? As a sponsor, which team would you allocate advertising dollars to? And as a franchise owner, how furious would you be that your own league sold away your exclusive rights?

Activision Blizzard's launch of *CoD* World League is controversial at best. It may benefit Activision Blizzard in the short term due to franchising revenues. But this doesn't make *CoD*'s league a good decision for *Overwatch*, its fans, or its teams.

LoL is likely here to stay. And unless *Overwatch* radically revisits its business model, and its relationship with the *CoD* World League, it will likely not succeed long term as an esport.

A VICTORY FOR VALOR?

As this book goes to print, Riot Games is preparing to launch its first ever FPS into closed beta: *Valorant*. So how does OMENS predict *Valorant* will perform?

Although the FPS market is crowded, *Valorant* is launching against a dated incumbent: CS:GO. And *Valorant* boasts needed (and difficult-to-clone) innovations, including integrated anti-cheat software and global, 128-tick servers (O). *Valorant* is free-to-play (M), and will leverage LoL's community (and eventually, its franchise structure) to catalyze fans (E). Furthermore, *Valorant* is optimized for even low-end PCs, enhancing virality (N).

But what about switching costs (S)? The core mechanics of FPS games are similar (aiming and shooting), and hence highly transferable. While *Valorant* adds heroic powers to the mix, it's nothing the genre hasn't seen before. Instead, *Valorant* aims to lock-in players with collectability. Unlike CS:GO, *Valorant* features unlockable heroes (or agents), each with their own unique abilities.

Overall, this author is bullish on *Valorant*. But he is nervous that its content pipeline may suffer from Riot's obsession with competitive balance. For example, *Valorant* is rumored to have only 12 agents available at launch (compared to LoL's original 40). If Riot can balance content cadence with competitive culture, the publisher may have a smash hit on their hands.

CHAPTER ELEVEN

VISUALIZING WAR

It's time to zoom out and see how the whole esports landscape fits together. Using the entire esports ecosystem (EEE) model, we'll visualize how all the disparate games and businesses we've discussed so far interact. And we'll learn how many of these companies are destined to come into conflict.

The EEE maps every esports business into one of six major categories:

- Publishers and games
- Leagues and tournaments
- Streaming and media platforms
- Teams and pros
- Digital gaming tools
- Physical gaming products

Publishers and games – The companies that develop, produce, and sell esports. For example, Riot Games makes *LoL*, so we see both logos front and center in this category.

Leagues and tournaments – The organizations through which gamers compete and win prizes. These can be game-specific, like the OWL, but there are also tournament platforms that exist to serve multiple titles independently. These multigame leagues tend to have a demographic specialization, such as CSL's focus on collegiate esports.

Streaming and media platforms – The means by which fans watch esports events. The largest streaming platform, Twitch, dominates this category.

Teams and pros – Largely analogous to traditional sports teams, the gamer organizations that compete in esports tournaments.

Digital gaming products – The digital tools that facilitate gaming. They are broken into four subcategories: training (helping gamers improve), connecting (helping gamers interact), wagering (betting on games), and content (gaming videos, news, and guides).

Physical gaming products – The consumer-packaged goods sold to esports fans around the world. Physical gaming products are grouped into subcategories: PCs and peripherals (gaming computers), and lifestyle and apparel products (jerseys).

Money flows into these categories from two sources: Gamers and fans collectively drive about $26 billion in spending, purchasing digital items, event tickets, and more.[1] And brands purchase advertising, media rights, and sponsorship, spending about $897 million annually.[2] (However, this category is growing up to 40 percent every year, explaining why many publishers create their own leagues. Advertising and sponsorship may eventually reach $40 billion or more, in line with traditional sports.[3])

The EEE landscape also features external pressures. Distribution platforms, like Steam and GameStop, are where consumers buy games. These encroach from the left because they primarily affect left-hand categories, in particular eroding publisher margins. (Explaining why many publishers, like Epic, Activision Blizzard, and Valve have launched their own sales platforms.) Similarly, independent authorities, like AnyKey, enforce fairness standards across esports. Authorities encroach from the right because they primarily impact right-hand categories, in particular regulating pros and teams.

The EEE's y-axis represents direct competition. In turn, the x-axis represents both partnership and diversification. Companies can collaborate across categories for mutual benefit (as Riot partners with Twitch to stream the LCS). Or companies can expand across categories into entirely new lines of business (as Activision Blizzard did by creating the OWL).

Crucially, the x-axis has a great chasm in it. It is difficult for companies to diversify across this gap, because of conflict of interest. For example, Activision Blizzard can't own a team in its OWL because of bias and favoritism. Similarly, Cloud9 can't make its own game and then compete in it.

The chasm is a fundamental divide in esports; a battle line between two distinct types of businesses: those seeking to *make competition* and those *built on competing*. And the two sides of the chasm are consolidating for battle...

The first EEE consolidation is occurring with publishers. Companies that make games are incredibly powerful, earning billions in revenue and employing thousands of coders, artists, and marketers. And publishers own their entire esport end-to-end. To appreciate how significant this is, imagine if the NBA owned basketball in the same way Riot owns *LoL*. Want to play a quick pickup game? You'll need to rent that court from the NBA. Need a ball? The NBA will sell it to you, and they're the

The Entire Esports Ecosystem

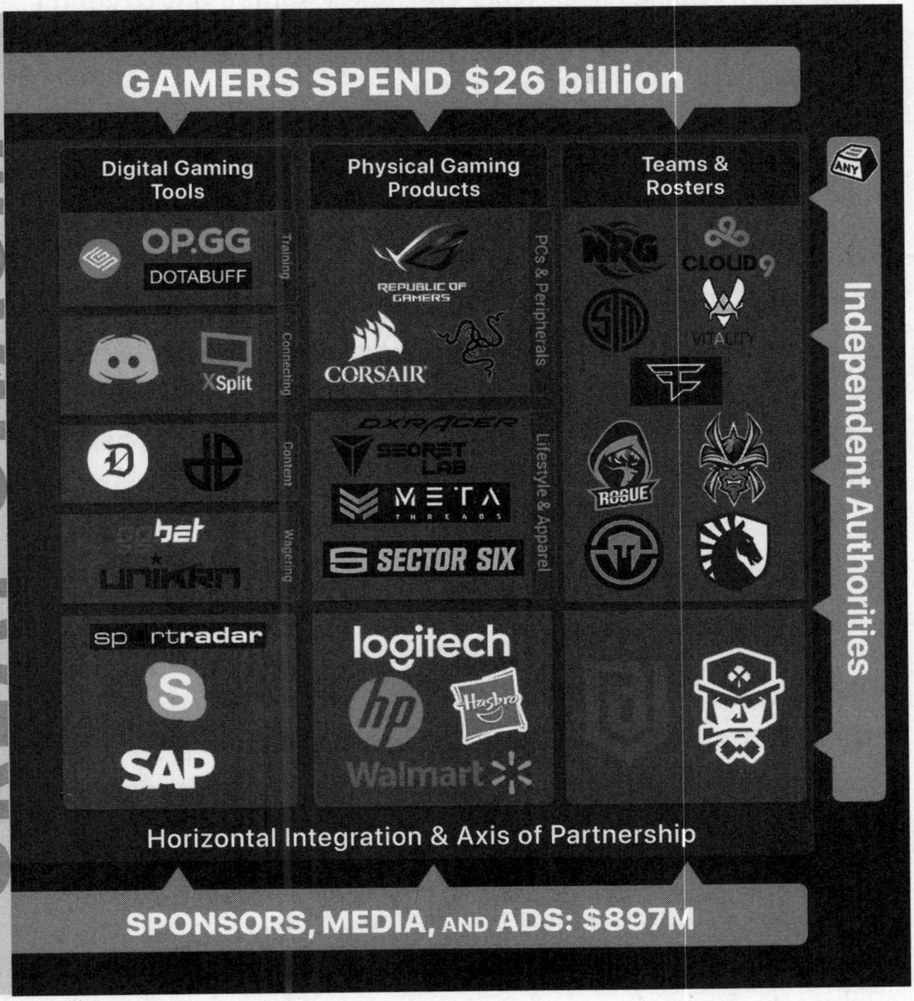

GAMERS SPEND $26 billion

Digital Gaming Tools

Physical Gaming Products

Teams & Rosters

ANY

Training

Connecting

Content

Wagering

PCs & Peripherals

Lifestyle & Apparel

Independent Authorities

GREAT CHASM

Horizontal Integration & Axis of Partnership

SPONSORS, MEDIA, AND ADS: $897M

only one who can. Don't like their price? Too bad. No one else can legally make basketballs. Need new equipment to compete in? Your jersey, your shoes, and everything else you wear are NBA-only products. There is literally no alternative.

Because publishers own everything, they can capture as much of the value their game creates as they choose. Historically, publishers have been happy to let other businesses host tournaments and stream events, collecting a licensing fee in return. But publishers don't have to. Because of the BAMS advertising and assets monetization model, more publishers are choosing to own their sport end-to-end (for example, Activision Blizzard creating the OWL and Riot creating the LCS). Media monetization causes two EEE categories—publishers and leagues—to merge.

We see a similar trend of competitive consolidation with streaming services. Today, Twitch is the dominant platform for esports media and hence advertising dollars. But as companies like Facebook (FB.gg), Google (YouTube Live), Microsoft (Mixer), and Fox (Caffeine) have entered the market, streaming platforms now compete over exclusive talent, much as broadcasters compete over TV shows. Most prominently, Mixer poached Tyler "Ninja" Blevins from Twitch, but there have been and will continue to be many high-profile defections.

But talent is just the tip of the iceberg. In esports, the ultimate form of exclusive content is the games themselves, and today, many streaming companies, like Microsoft and Amazon, already make games. More will follow. And scariest off all, Tencent owns both a Chinese streaming platform and massive stakes in key publishers (including 100 percent of Riot and 40 percent of Epic).[4] Eventually, publishers will make streaming their games exclusive to their own platforms, just as

TOO BIG TO FAIL?

The *A* in BAMS—assets and advertising—is also a risky monetization strategy for publishers because it's expensive to enter new media businesses. For example, Activision Blizzard had to create an entirely new esports division to support the OWL, costing tens of millions of dollars. As publishers spend more, they become increasingly leveraged against their game's success. And this leverage cascades across publishers. If Activision Blizzard spends $100 million to support *Call of Duty* esports, then Riot Games must spend *at least* that much to compete.

Increasing leverage means that an esport's failure will have increasingly devastating effects on its parent company. Already, the tepid success of the OWL has cut *half* the stock market value of Activision Blizzard across three years. Eventually, esports may go the way of the film industry. An unlucky publisher that strings together too many failures in sequence will fail.[5] This is another reason why the ketchup world from our last chapter is important: as esports stabilize, publishers can take fewer risks launching new properties, avoiding potentially devastating results.

Disney originally licensed its content to Netflix, but clawed it back to establish Disney+.

As a result, the left side of the EEE will converge. Streaming platforms will become publishers, and publishers will open leagues. The businesses of creating competition will merge.

A third and final consolidation will occur across teams. Unlike traditional sports, teams already operate in multiple games. A top organization like Team Liquid competes at the highest levels in *eleven* popular esports. This would be like the New York Yankees also fielding teams in the NBA, NFL, NHL, FIFA, and five other sports. Teams compete in multiple esports because of scale benefits: better advertising deals, more impressive training facilities, and fewer duplicated resources. Teams even purchase one another to capture this value, such as

WHERE IS THE REMOTE?

Notably absent from our discussion of streaming platforms is traditional TV. Flipping through channels at home, you might occasionally notice gaming tournaments broadcast alongside traditional sports. National stations such as TBS pair esports with mainstream entertainment offerings, and the OWL has often been featured prominently on ESPN.

But most esports fans watch online. Online streaming platforms distribute content freely, instantly, and interactively to any digital device. And they are perfect for targeted advertising, preferred by digitally savvy marketers at major corporations.

Perhaps the largest irony of the streaming war is that we already know its first casualty: cable media. Given the importance of sports to broadcast television, if you believe esports are the future of competition, or at least a significant part of it, then broadcasters have a gaping hole in their content pipeline.

Dignitas buying Clutch Gaming[6] or the Immortals taking over the Houston Outlaws.[7]

Large teams also achieve scale benefits through category diversification. Owning an apparel company might not make sense when you have only one pro roster. But when you have dozens, it's time to consider making your own gear. The same holds true for content production, gaming guides, and more. As a result, just as we see teams purchasing other teams, we observe teams buying into digital and physical gaming businesses, such as Immortals purchasing Gamers Club[8] or the New York Excelsior's owner launching their own clothing line.[9] The right-hand side of the EEE is consolidating, too.

Eventually, these megateams will seek conflict. Today, publishers hold all the power in esports. They can disband organizations at will,[10] shut off gaming services they dislike,[11] and farm up the price of product licenses.[12] Publishers can even levy taxes.[13, 14]

But scale is kryptonite to the publishers' superpower. Megateams can fight back, because losing a single roster or product won't matter amongst dozens. Instead, megateams will turn on publishers, arguing, "Look at the fandom I bring, the content I produce, the infrastructure I own. By being in your game, I make your game better. So start paying me for it!" We've already observed teams extracting such value from smaller esports titles.[15]

As a result, esports is on a collision course between the left- and right-hand sides of the EEE. And there is strong precedent for this in the history of traditional sports itself. Teams battled leagues during their formative years, just as with baseball's Players League in 1890.

The future of esports will be defined by consolidation and conflict, as megateams and diversifying publishers increasingly come into conflict across the chasm. And this is great news for esports fans. Because large-scale rivalry means more and better everything: content, prizing, innovation. Competition will be the fire that propels esports into the stratosphere over the next decade.

DO ESPORTS TEAMS COMPETE?

On the surface, esports teams appear competitive with one another. For example, the New York Excelsior vies with the Boston Uprising for the *Overwatch* Championship each season. But this conflict is banal. In reality, teams succeed or fail together based on the traction of their underlying league.

Let's illustrate this point with examples from traditional sports. The most valuable baseball team, the Yankees, is worth $5 billion. The least valuable, the Miami Marlins, is still worth $1 billion.[16] And both these valuations are a far cry higher than the most valuable MLS team (Atlanta United, worth $500 million).[17] The bigger the game, the more valuable every franchise competing in it. As a result, teams gain the most not by winning championships individually, but by growing their common league collectively. (The formation of Flashpoint, a recently announced league created by top *Counter-Strike: Global Offensive* pro teams, further underscores both this point and the coming conflict between publishers and megateams across the EEE.)

And baseball teams aren't worth billions just because baseball is popular. They are also valuable because MLB has granted exclusive baseball rights to these teams. As a result, teams are also incentivized to collectively negotiate better rights deals with their parent league to capture more value. It's one thing if a single organization asks for greater revenue share; it's another if every team in that league collectively bargains for it.

The financial incentives to collectively promote and bargain mean that teams don't truly compete with one another. In fact, most cooperate, creating yet another force driving industry consolidation and publisher conflict.

PART III
A NEW CHALLENGER APPEARS!

CHAPTER TWELVE

FLAWLESS VICTORY

What will be the next big esport? We've seen how quickly new genres of competitive gaming can be created, such as *PUBG* innovating BRs. Are other seismic shifts in the esports landscape coming?

The answer is a resounding yes.

There is a new class of esport enjoying a groundswell of interest right now, and unlike existing genres of competitive gaming, this innovation has the potential to turn every single video game into esports. Even the original *Super Mario Bros.*

And we're going to explore this new genre by telling the story of one gamer's quest to achieve the impossible: a truly flawless victory.

Faraaz Khan was born in 1990 in Calgary, Canada, into a family of engineers who had fled war-stricken Bangladesh seeking a better life. But despite his family's relative affluence—and their luck in escaping the political collapse of their home country—Faraaz's childhood was not a happy one. His parents soon divorced, and his father quickly remarried.

Faraaz remembers growing up unmoored. "It was a really unhappy childhood," he explains. "I was really lonely because of my family circumstances. I didn't have many friends or family support. A lot of things kids usually learn in the home, I had to teach myself."

Faraaz had a favorite uncle, a computer scientist and lifelong gamer who'd been playing since the original Atari. At his suggestion, Faraaz got into the hobby, starting "before I can remember, honestly." Digital worlds quickly became a refuge. "I'd find myself playing more and more. It was sort of like an escape for me, especially when things at home were tough."

By the time Faraaz turned thirteen, his parents worried that gaming had become an addiction. Returning from one of his frequent business trips, his father instilled his first and only parental rule: one hour of gaming per day.

"I cried more than I had ever cried in my entire life," Faraaz remembers. "Games truly mattered to me, and I saw my father's rule as taking a primary source of comfort and happiness in my life and applying arbitrary limits. Despite doing well in school, my anchor was made less accessible. I closed off further from the people around me."

For every parent who has ever wondered whether their child spends too much time gaming, Faraaz believes his life story is a counterpoint: "I know gaming was good for me," he says. "It may sound strange, but I loved it so much because it was teaching me. I learned morality from role-playing games, and the importance of perseverance from platformers like Mario. Games taught me many things about myself and developed me in ways that weren't happening in either my school or home life."

Perhaps Faraaz instinctively knew something that science is beginning to confirm: video games *can* be good for you. Research increasingly shows that gaming develops skills like patience, delayed gratification, perseverance, creative thinking, and strategic planning. Gaming can also help deal with depression and anxiety. All these may be reasons why even CNBC reports that playing games can help children get into college.[1]

"You can't look at gaming as time wasted," Faraaz explains. "Certainly some gaming can be. But not the way I played, and not the way a lot of gamers play. If you are learning, if you are engaging with the medium, it can be as valuable as any other human experience."

Eventually, whether in spite of or because of gaming, Faraaz earned himself admission to the University of Calgary. Free of parental supervision for the first time, a new existential question weighed on him. "What did I want to do with my life? I was under enormous pressure to figure it out. There was no question in my family that I should become an engineer, but I didn't want that type of regimented, nine-to-five job. I just couldn't see myself being happy."

One night, while searching through internet forums for tips on gaming, Faraaz stumbled onto a popular *StarCraft II* stream by Sean "Day9" Plott (who similarly inspired Amnesiac). "I found myself watching Day9 just being himself. He was playing games and having a great time. I thought: I could do that. And then I thought: I *want* to do that."

In late 2014, Faraaz won $3,500 playing blackjack at a Las Vegas casino. This money seeded his first streaming setup: "A dual-monitor PC, c920 webcam, blue snowball microphone, and capture card for my Wii U. I spent everything," Faraaz jokes. "The works. But the truth is I probably didn't have to. Streaming can be really cheap to get into. Today, I think it's possible for anyone with a computer, mic, and camera to become famous."

The accessibility of esports is a crucial aspect of its appeal, but it also results in a crowded marketplace that can make it difficult for new streamers to find an audience. Faraaz realized quickly that he needed to stand out.

"Twitch didn't become a proper job right away," he explains. "It was a struggle to build traction for my channel. At the same time, I worked at a Muay Thai gym, actively training and fighting, while also maintaining a full engineering course load at the University of Calgary. At night I would race to stream as much as I could because I loved it, but I started to worry it wouldn't become the career I'd hoped."

By late 2015, Faraaz still hadn't quite found his niche. So one night, browsing other streamers online to see what content was trending, he came upon a gamer called The_Happy_Hob playing a popular *Dark Souls* video game with a unique twist: Hob was trying to beat the game without getting hit. To contrast, an average player completing a *Dark Souls* title is struck about 50,000 times, if they can finish the game at all.

"I was amazed," Faraaz confesses. "The way Hob moved his avatar, the patience and discipline. It was masterful."

Faraaz's discovery came at a fortuitous time: the newest game in the series, *Dark Souls III*, was slated to launch in just a few short months. Games on Twitch always attract the most viewers at launch; Faraaz saw an opportunity to embrace Hob's challenge, and hopefully build his fandom by mastering *Dark Souls III*.

"I was going to be the first person in the world to beat that game without getting hit. That was that."

At launch in early 2016, only three people were crazy enough to dedicate themselves to no-hitting *Dark Souls III*: The_Happy_Hob, Squillakilla, and Faraaz Khan.

Starting on April 12, Faraaz began regimented practice: two hours offline, followed by an eight-hour livestream. His rivals adopted similar schedules. But after their long nights of grinding were over, rather than argue or ignore each other, the three came together to try to advance their study of *Dark Souls III*.

"What we were doing at the time was considered impossible," he explains. "Initially, the best any of us could do was to beat the game while getting hit maybe two hundred, three hundred times. But the crazy thing is we knew early on it was technically feasible to complete the perfect run. Each time we played, we got hit a little less because we came together and developed new strategies. We were breaking the game down into its fundamental components, figuring out exactly what could and could not be done in the pursuit of mastery. It was like a PhD program in *Dark Souls III*."

Surprisingly, the collaborative competitive environment Faraaz experienced is commonplace today. Because single-player games like *Dark Souls III* are deterministic experiences, albeit very elaborate ones, it is possible to—just like a scientist—research outcomes. As a result, seemingly archaic movements, carefully sequenced button inputs, and other so-called "strats" (short for strategies) can manipulate both a game's AI and random-number-generating systems. The result is that precision play—sometimes requiring inputs as accurate as one-sixtieth of a second—can result in perfectly consistent outcomes, and sometimes even logic-defying glitches.

April turned to May, then June, and something incredible happened.

"We started to get close," Faraaz recalls. "Like, we were having runs where we would get hit maybe five or six times. With every part of the game having been completed with no-hit elegance at some point, we knew *someone* was going to get it. All that was left was to put it all together. No-hit running didn't exist

TESTING THE TAS

In order to discover the limits of video games, some devotees create tool-assisted speedruns (TASs). Creating a TAS involves using an emulator, a specialized PC program used to emulate a game and monitor its memory in a controllable environment. Emulators allow TAS creators to test and retest millions of game inputs, often frame by frame, in order to optimize a "theoretically perfect" playthrough of a title. Many TASs are then console-verified, a process that involves replaying the optimized inputs on the game's original hardware to prove the perfect run is truly possible.

While TASing does involve using emulators for testing, it's important to note that TASs don't hack or alter the original game to achieve their phenomenal results. In layman's terms: TASs don't cheat. However, the fact that the playthroughs produced by TASs are *theoretically* possible doesn't mean they are *humanly* possible. Often TASs require levels of precision beyond even the most dedicated gamers, such as maintaining frame-accurate inputs for hours in order to manipulate a game's random-number-generating systems. Nonetheless, TASs are incredibly valuable resources for people seeking to master games, since they often uncover new strategies or techniques. And sometimes, tricks at first deemed humanly impossible are later found to have human-viable setups.

Many consider TAS runs to be works of art; they are certainly works of entertainment. Some of the most famous TASs cover classic titles like *Super Metroid* and *Mario 64*. Because these playthroughs are so optimized, they are incredibly short. (So check them out if you're curious to see what games look like if played at the theoretical limits of machine-assisted perfection.)

formally yet in the gaming community, so when people watched us play, they *loved* it. We were creating something new."

As Faraaz neared the perfect *Dark Souls III* run, his popularity on Twitch soared. "Every day I streamed, more people came to watch me struggle. The rivalry between myself, Hob, and Squilla fed a kind of manic interest. The gaming internet as a whole was obsessed with *Dark Souls* back then. And suddenly, the idea of these three gamers, racing to achieve absolute perfection, caught on."

By mid-June, the margin of victory had narrowed to only two hits. But over the course of each two-hour-and-twenty-seven-minute run, the typical time required to complete *Dark Souls III*, the difference between one error and none loomed astronomical.

To put Faraaz's challenge into perspective, a *Dark Souls III* no-hit run is the gaming equivalent of an endurance marathon and a concert piano recital rolled into one. Completing a hitless run requires inputting precision commands requiring accuracy often measured in microseconds to defeat or avoid thousands of enemies with hundreds of unique attack patterns across dozens of maps, all for 150 minutes straight. Faraaz explains, "It's like walking a tightrope for two hours while balancing dozens of spinning plates—but the plates suddenly change in size and weight with each new in-game event. It is really, really hard."

Such mechanical proficiency seems superhuman.

"But I realized at a certain point, I was good enough," Faraaz says. "The barrier was psychological preparation. I knew to get the no-hit run I had to be mentally ready, not just technically proficient."

Faraaz combined well-researched mental discipline techniques along with the rigorous competitor's mindset he'd honed with Muay Thai kickboxing. He instilled a strict regime of sleep, meditation, and exercise. He constantly practiced "visioning" exercises, meditating on desired outcomes while mentally accepting failures as necessary for growth. As the perfect run neared, he tempered himself with ancient introspection techniques like a Vipassana retreat, which involved not speaking for ten days while meditating for sixteen hours or more. "It may sound strange to some people that I was meditating over a video game. But these techniques have existed for thousands of years to instill mental discipline and clarity. I was using them just as they were intended."

And, of course, Faraaz practiced *Dark Souls III*. A lot. "Every day I would wake up and defeat each boss, in sequence, ten times without getting hit. There are fourteen bosses required to complete a *Dark Souls III* no-hit run. That means I would complete one hundred forty perfect boss fights. If I got hit once, I would reset my counter for that boss. I had periods where I wouldn't sleep for thirty-six hours because I kept messing up a sequence or was resetting runs. But I kept going. It was just like being a kid, and how gaming taught me perseverance. I had to give everything to achieve my goal."

In the final days, the competition grew nerve-shatteringly close. "Any minute, any one of us—Squilla, Hob, or myself—could claim the title. I'd go to bed at night and be unable to sleep from the pressure. Total insomnia. And then when I finally did crash, I'd *literally* dream about practicing *Dark Souls III*. But the really weird part is I *wanted* my competitors to beat me. Squilla and Hob were great people, working just as hard as I was. Even though I had never met them in person up to this point, I felt strongly about their right to the title. So part of me hoped they'd win. And part of me had a heart attack every time they neared a perfect game."

In late June, Hob kicked a run that made it to Twin Princes—the second-to-final boss—without getting hit. He dropped that attempt, but Faraaz saw the success as a line in the sand. "I knew Hob would get it soon. And I knew it had to be me instead."

So the next day, Faraaz returned home from working an eight-hour shift in construction. His body ached, and his left leg spasmed from a minor injury. He had to be back on site early the next morning, but instead of resting, he booted up *Dark Souls III*.

One hour of attempts became two, then ten. "Something kept me playing that night. I was so tired I could barely see straight. But in a way that helped. It was all muscle memory at that point. It was about not getting in my own way; finding a state where I could play while being completely present and without self-sabotage. I knew if I thought about it, my mind would waste energy elsewhere and I would lose the run."

After gaming the entire night, Faraaz managed a run that hit Twin Princes around 9:02 a.m. "There was a moment when the boss teleported behind me, and I had to execute a microsecond roll from an attack off camera. Nine times out of ten, you get hit by that stuff. The run dies. But I didn't get hit. Princes went down. It's weird to say, but I knew I had completed the no-hit run then. The last boss, Cinder, is a lot harder than Twin Princes. But something about getting across that wall—about being at the final obstacle—meant everything was in reach."

At 9:08 a.m., Faraaz Khan became the first person ever to complete a no-hit run for *Dark Souls III*. Watching reruns of his stream that night, you can see Faraaz's fandom absolutely explode. "Take my energy! Take my energy! Take my energy!" fills his Twitch chat, an almost spiritual affirmation of success. Faraaz beams with radiant humility. The only words he can muster: "I did it. I did it. *I did it.*"

Just a few short months later, Faraaz Khan's grind continued. He next completed *Dark Souls III* with all optional content without getting hit, an even more incredible feat requiring an additional hour of precision play. And finally, in early 2017, Faraaz did the unthinkable: He became the first person in the world to beat every single *Dark Souls* game, and their spinoff *Bloodborne*, without getting hit.

Faraaz had finally earned his flawless victory.

"I mean, I don't think I'm that good at games," he confesses.

"I think what I am is disciplined and dedicated. I think I am a person who can set myself a task, and stick with it until I complete that task."

In the process of mastering these games, Faraaz had built a community of tens of thousands of fans following him on Twitch. His no-hit runs have been viewed millions of times on YouTube.

"It's a dream for me," he says. "That being good at gaming became my career."

Esports can be more than team-based, head-to-head experiences. Faraaz and his rivals pioneered another path to rewarding digital skill: challenge running.

Faraaz took a traditional single-player video game, not designed to be an esport, and added rules and stipulations to make the game into a competitive experience. In essence, Faraaz invented digital weightlifting. He and his fellow hitless runners took a solitary challenge and added higher and higher hurdles—more and more weight—that fewer and fewer people could clear. In doing so, Faraaz turned a regular game into a competitive experience.

Faraaz's pioneering no-hit runs emerged in parallel with another type of challenge gaming: speedrunning.

Speedrunning finds its roots in the early 1990s, when fans of the original *Doom* raced to complete that title, or various segments thereof, as fast as possible. Speedrunning's most famous early achievement was *Quake* Done Quick, a hybridized recording of the fastest individual level completion times, which finished the legendary FPS in under twenty minutes.[2] Just as Faraaz invented digital weightlifting, speedrunners created the digital equivalent of sprinting.

In early 2014, the newly created website speedrun.com skyrocketed to popularity. Today, the speedrunning community consists of close to 175,000 gamers and nearly a million qualified runs across 14,000 games. Twice every year, these gamers join together for the Games Done Quick marathon, which raised over $5 million for charity in 2019.[3]

"What is happening right now," explains Allison "Skybilz" Maino, a prominent speedrunner and esports pro, "is that we are actively broadening the definition of esports. Speedrunning and no-hit running are two sides of the same coin. They are all part of a bigger community, which goes by many names, including challenge running. But the common idea is the same: setting constraints on games—time limits, input restrictions, save limitations, and more—to make any title competitive. And this, in turn, transforms any game into an esport."

Will challenge running affect esports as a whole? Drastically.

The biggest implication of challenge running is that popular non-esports titles can be given an extended shelf life through esports. This opportunity is particularly valuable to publishers like Nintendo, who enjoy limited esports presence outside of fighting games. Challenge running potentially makes any video game more enduring through a constant stream of fresh challenges. Many publishers now encourage this behavior, most often by building customizable speedrunning modes into their games.

But the primary benefit of challenge running is accessibility. Because traditional esports are based around direct conflict, games are often violent. Even cartoonish *Overwatch* and *Fortnite* are still fundamentally about shooting people in the head. But because challenge running is focused on individual improvement (or personal bests, as the community refers to them), it allows for competition in friendlier games. Now *Sonic* the Hedgehog, *Super Mario*, and more can be reinvigorated with high-stakes tournaments.

The broad accessibility of challenge running appeals to family brands. Disney, in particular, would like to cultivate esports' demographics but not esports' content. The company simply can't put shotguns on the same network as *The Lion King*, even if it's what tweens want to watch. But challenge running gives Disney, and similar businesses, a way to square the circle by featuring competitive gaming without endorsing violence. It is this accessibility that drove Disney to launch esports on its XD television network with *ESL Speedrunners*.[4]

"You are going to see more household brands investing in

WHAT'S A FIGHTING GAME?

In fighting games, players control a single character from a side view, on either a 2D or 3D plane, as they engage in one-on-one combat. By inputting strict sequences of timed button presses, players perform special moves and attack combinations for additional damage.

In some ways, fighting games *were* the birth of esports, with the original *Street Fighter* and its sequels dominating arcades with iconic characters like Ryu, Chun-Li, and Ken. However, over time, fighters have eroded in popularity, largely due to accessibility. The strict system of button combination that makes fighters skill-intensive also renders them unwieldy and frustrating for many gamers. Additionally, the difficulty of fighting games is arbitrary, with developers intentionally making attacks obtuse as an easy path to increasing their title's skill ceiling.

One fighting game that stands above the rest is *Super Smash Brothers* (*SSB*). *SSB* is Nintendo's only popular esport, and it's a hit for a reason. *SSB* intentionally eschews difficult button combinations; its core attacks are easily queued, providing immediate gratification to new players. *SSB* also features a rich roster of Nintendo's beloved characters, further broadening the game's accessibility. Despite the success of a few marquee fighting tournaments like Evo and Shine, over all fighting games have not approached the popularity of more traditional esports like *LoL*.

speedrunning and challenge-driven gaming, because it's a great way to produce esports content that's suitable for the whole family," Skybilz explains. "In fact, it is literally the only way for many G-rated brands to authentically participate in esports. And as runners, we are aware of the broad appeal of our community. It's why most of our major tournaments feature very strict language-use guidelines, for example, to avoid the negativity that can dominate traditional esports."

Challenge running also broadens esports' appeal to older viewers. Gamers who grew up with the original Nintendo, for example, may have difficulty orienting themselves in the frenetic landscape of a *Fortnite* free-for-all. But in challenge running communities, old games are hugely popular precisely because they are *classic*. For example, the original *Super Mario Bros.* remains one of the most popular speedrunning games, with a ludicrously fast and heavily contested world record (the entire game has been completed in four minutes and fifty-five seconds).[5]

At the time of this writing, challenge running is in an embryonic phase, with its popularity still small compared to traditional esports like *Overwatch* or *Hearthstone*. However, challenge running offers incredible value to both publishers (extended revenues) and gamers (accessibility), ensuring future investment in the genre. Already, major esports venues and pro teams are making significant commitments to the space.[6,7]

In the years ahead, challenge running will play an integral part of esports' evolution. Just as television started with news programming, but quickly expanded into Saturday morning cartoons, so too will esports embrace and elevate its most accessible content format. And that is great news for parents. Because their children are going to need all the practice they can get to earn those coveted esports collegiate scholarships we're about to discuss.

CHAPTER THIRTEEN

THE NEW KID AT SCHOOL

College athletics occupies an important place in the modern sporting landscape. It's where professionals cut their teeth on the big stage. And where universities rake in billions in profit. College sports create stories of lifechanging success and fandoms that unite generations of alumni.

So why should it be any different for esports?

In this chapter, we're going to explore how today, right now, esports are taking over higher education. From major degrees to varsity letters, esports have quickly come to define campus life in a way that is forcing academia to take notice, in some sense becoming the front line of modern society's awakening to digital gaming.

And it all began with a guy called Kurt and a simple dream.

"I just knew right from the beginning. It had to exist," explains Kurt Melcher, the "godfather" of collegiate esports.

Back in 2013, Melcher was the associate athletics director of Robert Morris University (RMU). He was an administrator and coach who loved gaming in his spare time.

"I played *League of Legends* every night and most of my opponents were college kids," Kurt says. "Over voice chat, I'd hear how much esports meant to them. The way they described gaming sounded just like an athlete raving about sports."

Something clicked in Kurt. He compared his daily profession of coaching to his nightly hobby of gaming, and couldn't escape the conclusion that the two belonged together. "I remembered my own collegiate sports career. Institutional training not only developed me as an athlete, but made me a stronger scholar and a better person. I saw all the same positives in esports. All the same benefits. Games are deeply competitive experiences, teaching commitment, loyalty, trust, practice, and focus. I realized everything I learned from college athletics could be taught through esports. So I knew I had to bring varsity esports to college. It was never a question of if I was right. I knew I was. It was a question of if I could get Robert Morris—or any school, for that matter—to listen."

And so Kurt began his quixotic quest to create the world's first varsity esports program.

"At first I didn't tell many people about my plan," he says. "I took notes, refined ideas. At some point I remember discussing things with my wife. I thought she was going to have me committed. But instead she gave me the courage to bring my ideas forward. She told me: 'Why should only the kids who put a ball in a goal be the ones to earn scholarship money?' We have these normative assumptions about athletics, so we don't think it's strange that a kid who is good at swinging a bat gets a free ride. But if you really think about it, what's so special about football? About soccer? About lacrosse? Why shouldn't other competitive endeavors be worthy of scholarship?"

Kurt sought guidance from a mentor at Robert Morris, his boss, Megan Smith. Her advice was to communicate his ideas to RMU's presidential board, but in a format the school would be comfortable reviewing.

"Basically, I needed to draft a white paper," explains Kurt. "The first-ever white paper in the world on college esports."

Kurt got to work. Between his daily duties at the college and nightly games of *LoL*, he began researching, studying, and interviewing. There was no blueprint for college esports. He literally had to figure out what varsity gaming should look like from square one.

"I just took things to their logical conclusion," he says. "And a few months later the white paper was finished. It was only as I was reading it over that I realized how ambitious it was. And by ambitious, I mean certifiably insane."

What exactly was Kurt's vision? Complete and utter commitment.

"The white paper demanded total support, at the same level as RMU supported every other collegiate athletic activity," Kurt explains. "That meant we needed a facility. We needed staff. We needed to start recruiting. With scholarship dollars, mind you. And scholarship dollars that were the equal of basketball, or baseball, or soccer. And that meant we needed equipment. And jerseys. Meals after games, celebrations. You name it. Everything that was *understood* as par for the course in traditional athletics, we needed for esports. Because they are fundamentally the same thing. Of course all of this came with a big price tag. An entirely new budget line item on the college bankroll. We didn't even have a *club* for esports at Robert Morris at the time."

But Kurt believed. His plan drafted, he walked into the president of RMU's office on a chilly Friday morning, nervously envisioning being laughed out of the room.

"I launched into my white paper, describing computer needs and tournament preparations, and in return I was getting these glassy-eyed stares," Kurt says. "I realized I was starting at square one, when I needed to begin at square zero. I needed to explain what an esport was."

He remembers leaving that first meeting with a mixture of fear and uncertainty. But also hope. He hadn't been laughed out of the room. He had been listened to.

"Things were left very open-ended. I had no idea what was going to happen, until the proposal was called back for a second review. And here I give full credit to the president of Robert Morris, and every other faculty member on that board. They are why Robert Morris earned its place in esports history. The board had really done their homework. They hadn't understood what esports was, but they had tried to appreciate the vision. And they saw what a new class of sport might mean for RMU."

Robert Morris's board was likely the first of any major academic institution to appreciate the unique type of student engagement offered by esports. "Competitive gaming has the power to reach a new class of student," explains Kurt. "Esports touches someone who maybe doesn't have an interest in traditional athletics, or a cappella groups, or Greek life. It brings the university, its brand, and its positive influence into a wholly new sphere of student life. And this type of engagement strongly correlates with better academic performance and higher graduation rates."

Varsity esports might bring other benefits to RMU as well. At many universities, baseball, football, and basketball teams drive admissions numbers. If a new type of sport existed, unique to Robert Morris, it could be a significant point of advantage when sourcing students.

Additionally, esports might buoy collegiate funding. More students would mean higher admissions revenue, of course. But there was also a bigger picture. "Traditional sports are big drivers of alumni giving," explains Kurt. "Finances were never a core motivator for RMU to engage with esports, but the possibility of new revenues certainly existed, because esports had the potential to catalyze an entirely new category of alumni to give."

In the meeting, Kurt felt the passion and the excitement the board had for his vision, but he saw they still struggled to believe in esports. That just because esports *might* happen, didn't mean it *should* happen right now.

"I remember the exact moment I convinced the president of RMU. I had an iPad with me and an LCS [*League of Legends* Championship Series] match queued up. I wanted to show him what an esports competition looked like. To be amazed at its size and scale," Kurt explains. "So I replayed this LCS game, with its thousands of live fans. With casters and analysts; spotlights and replays; a massive production budget. The president was stunned. I could almost read his mind, because I saw the recognition: 'This is ESPN.' Esports isn't dissimilar to watching baseball or football. It was new, but also familiar."

Shortly after that meeting, Kurt received his green light. And just like that, Robert Morris University became the first school ever to offer a varsity esports program. Fully funded, signed, and sealed.

But there was a problem. How in the world was anybody going to find out about RMU's new endeavor? And, more to the point, was anybody going to care?

Kurt and the rest of his burgeoning esports staff labored in a kind of half-life for the next few months; an open secret of uncertainty. They built out their space, hired their coaches, and designed and branded their jerseys, all while wondering, *if we build it, will they come?*

And they came like lightning.

"I'd reached out to Riot Games [the makers of *LoL*], just to let them know what RMU was planning," Kurt says. "In truth, I wanted to get Riot's okay. I didn't want the first big event in our program to be a lawsuit from a billion-dollar company. To be honest, I think Riot had trouble believing what RMU was doing. They were like, 'Okay, you're a student at this school?' And I was like, 'No, I'm an athletic director.' They couldn't wrap their heads around it. Our first correspondence was through support tickets, as if I was troubleshooting a technical problem with the game. But Riot kept talking. Eventually they understood. And they loved the commitment RMU had made so much, they decided to put our program on the front of the *League of Legends* client—the application everyone has to open to start a game of *LoL*. I mean, I always believed there would be interest in varsity esports. But I'd prepared myself for a few PR items, maybe a couple hundred new applications. But that day, within twenty-four hours, we got thirty thousand prospective students reaching out to Robert Morris. It was unbelievable. My life changed forever."

"Riot had warned: 'Our game is pretty popular, brace yourself.' But I didn't take them seriously. I certainly don't think anyone else at the college believed the response would be so huge. At that point, they were barely trusting me. But after Riot made our program public, we became the leading institution for varsity esports in the world. Within a week, everyone was reaching out to us: HBO, CNN, the *Wall Street Journal*, the *New York Times*, the BBC. It was a media firestorm."

"It changed the university completely," Kurt concludes. "RMU has always been a great school, but this put us on the map in a different way. It became our point of difference, and an international draw for our student body. Needless to say, the college was very happy with my proposal after that."

Barely five years after RMU kicked off its first varsity program, the collegiate landscape for esports has transformed. Today, 60 percent or more of US colleges have a dedicated esports club or more formal program. "I think the number is closer to one hundred percent, it's just difficult to document," explains Tim Loew, founding administrator of Becker College's esports program. "Full-time colleges specializing in esports have opened in China, Japan, and Europe. It is estimated that over fifty percent of college students play competitive games. On a typical Friday night, the only thing consuming more bandwidth on university servers is Netflix."

And as esports infiltrated athletics, it also spread into academia.

"We knew we had to be first to introduce a major," says Alan Ritacco of Becker College. "We actually looked at what RMU had done for varsity sports as an example. Becker is already a premier college ranked in the top three in the world for interactive media game design. So why not take esports into academia?"

By 2018, colleges around the world, including UCI, Emerson, and more, had started offering selected classes on esports. But Becker College took things a step further by creating the first-ever bachelor's degree in esports management in the US, a feat that has since been copied over a dozen times, becoming arguably the fastest expanding frontier of higher education.

"Why can't you teach esports as a business?" Tim Loew suggests. "We have a sports management major. We have art and design majors. Programming majors. Competitive gaming, if you think about it, is the most naturally academic subject of all because it incorporates these fields of study, and many more. It is the first truly interdisciplinary profession in the world. That's actually the biggest challenge of teaching esports. It's just so sprawling, there are so many different ways you can attack it. We've picked a few angles, like management, but our approach isn't necessarily the only way, or the right way. You can cut this however you want."

Kurt adds: "You see cross-curricula integration in traditional sports all the time. For example, kinesiology has student trainers embedded alongside teams, building real-life experience. Media students are involved in the athletic department, covering games. Mathematics majors might data mine new sabermetrics insights with the help of the baseball team. All these synergies are turbocharged in esports because the industry touches so many disciplines. In that regard, I think traditional sports are *disadvantaged* compared to esports."

Just as esports is infiltrating college academia, it also reaches younger still in our education system. The "Friday night lights"

Becker College esports students training on campus.[7]

are just as real in esports as they are in football. And gaming needs a feeder system for its growing collegiate interest. As a result, high school esports are exploding too.

In 2019 alone, PlayVS raised close to $100 million to develop a high school esports ecosystem.[1] The startup reports 68 percent of US high schools are forming teams in preparation for its leagues.[2] And similar businesses are springing up in China, Japan, Korea, Germany, the UK, and elsewhere.

The esports academic revolution is here, and it's no longer limited to college. It's threading itself into every nook and cranny that sport itself occupies. We're not there yet, but there is fast coming a day when you might be taking your kindergartener to *LoL* practice.

But there is a potential roadblock to the success of esports in academia: the National Collegiate Athletic Association (NCAA). The NCAA serves as the governing body overseeing all sports at university campuses across the United States. And in April 2019, the NCAA voted to *not* incorporate college esports (at least in the near future).[3] Prior to this decision, NCAA President Mark Emmert opined: "We know that some of the content [in games] is really violent. We don't particularly embrace games where the objective is to blow your opponent's head off. We know there are serious concerns about health and wellness around those games."[4]

So will the NCAA's decision to ignore esports hold back their adoption on college campuses, particularly given the violence concerns raised by President Emmert?

Not at all.

"Esports will happen regardless. This is just a mistake on the behalf of the NCAA," explains Tim Loew. "In an age when their relevance is being challenged by regulatory pushback, they need to be positioning themselves at the forefront of student life. In my view, this decision may end up contributing to the decline of the NCAA. It has opened the door for a competitor to govern esports across college campuses."

And this has already happened. The National Association of Collegiate Esports (NACE) was cofounded by Kurt Melcher in 2016. Already, NACE plays the role of the NCAA on over 300 college campuses and growing.

However, the NCAA's failure to adopt esports has had one negative effect on college esports: fragmentation.

"Because the NCAA hesitated, the esports landscape has remained disunified. The NCAA would have given every school an immediate and universal standard to rally around for esports, because that standard was already present on every campus in America," explains Kurt. "I cofounded NACE as a solution to this void, but I'll be the first to admit that the organization is relatively new. And there is such rapid adoption of esports, sometimes schools don't even know we exist or how best to work with us. That's the biggest threat to college esports today: the gap in esports education amongst college administrators. I got lucky at Robert Morris because the university was willing to learn. But most schools around America, and the world, are jumping into esports not because of understanding, but due to fear. They see a trend and know they need to be a part of it. The education gap amongst academic faculty is the single biggest barrier to the adoption of college esports."

Tim Loew adds, "It's not helped by how invisible esports can be. If you're playing esports it's not like you need to be out on a field somewhere. Competitive gaming happens in dorm rooms, often late at night."

"And gaming itself is fragmented, too," interjects Kurt. "There are *so many* subgroups, because there are so many games. Your college may have a *massive* esports presence, but you might not realize it because it is segmented by game: *Smash Brothers* Club, *League of Legends* Club, *StarCraft* Club."

"That's why I think it's so hard for administrators to understand," Kurt concludes. "There is no way to fund esports. Just like there's no way to fund sports. You need to know the games you are competing in, the level of competition you are targeting, the match roles you are recruiting for, and more. And that knowledge barrier is really hard to cross."

But although the ride might be bumpy, Kurt sees the future of collegiate esports as just as inevitable as when he first wrote his white paper for RMU.

"It comes down to a school's mission," he explains. "Universities exist to help students fulfill their dreams. And esports is a dream millions of college applicants hold dear. That's why schools are figuring out esports. Not because it's easy. But because it's the future."

As more and more colleges embrace esports, the reward for getting good at games increases. Because now even amateur enthusiasts can benefit through educational stipends and scholarships. Just as collegiate athletics provides an interim milestone for millions of aspiring sportsmen, so too has esports begun to reward its youngest fans.

CHAPTER FOURTEEN

A LEAGUE OF THEIR OWN

If the goal of esports is to be like traditional sports—to become permanent, intergenerational competitive experiences—then are esports a *threat* to sports?

Baseball, football, and other traditional sports don't play nice. Each competes for mindshare, wallet spend, and more. While fans can be devotees of multiple sports, the NBA Finals and the Super Bowl aren't broadcast on the same day for a reason: They are direct competitors. As one sport rises in popularity, it usually comes at the expense of others.

The best example of this is baseball and football. In the 1960s, baseball reigned supreme as the king of US sports, with 34 percent of Americans citing it as their favorite pastime.[1] Fast forward to today, and only 9 percent of Americans claim baseball as their favorite. What caused this transition? Football's surge in popularity.

Today, the NFL makes about six times more than MLB in advertising revenues alone. It is the Super Bowl, not the World Series, that dominates marketing budgets and media attention annually.

So what caused football to conquer its competition? Television. As radio declined in prominence, football embraced

Share of Playoff Advertising Spend
2018

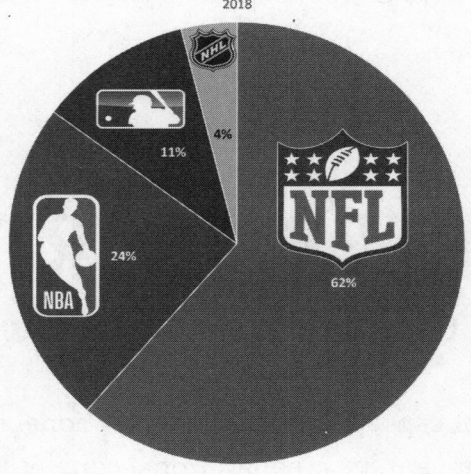

Because of surging popularity, the NFL in 2019 was about six times more popular with advertisers than MLB.

TV. It was the first sport to launch instant replays, onscreen visualization tools, and more.[2] Tastes changed, and the NFL more effectively adapted to the media revolution.

So if the NFL can dethrone MLB, can esports take down the NFL?

As we've already established, esports are incredibly popular. So popular, in fact, that they already eclipse traditional sports. As early as 2017, viewership for major esports events like ESL One outpaced the World Series. And in 2019, the LCS was watched by more people than the Super Bowl![3]

Compared to sports viewers, esports spectators are both younger and more international. This foretells a bright future: as foreign markets grow, and younger viewers grow up, esports should further increase in popularity. And given its attractive audience size and demographics, esports is already competing directly with traditional sports for advertisers' wallets.

So how are traditional sports fighting back?

⚽

In 1987, Eddie Dombrower and Don Daglow, the designers of the 1983 Intellivision hit *World Series Baseball*, set out to produce a sequel. Rather than rely on their own fan-level knowledge, they hired a guru: Earl Weaver, manager of the Baltimore Orioles. The resulting game was a smash hit and was immediately followed by *John Madden Football*. This subsequent success inspired publisher Electronic Arts to launch the EA Sports brand in 1991.

Today, EA Sports is a digital powerhouse, producing franchise games for FIFA, the NHL, and the NFL. With rival publisher 2K Games helming the NBA license, all traditional sports leagues now boast bestselling crossover video games.

These games are critically important to their parent leagues. They generate *a lot* of revenue. The *FIFA* series, for example, has sold 260 million copies worldwide, generating billions in income for the FIFA franchise.[4] But they matter to more than just a league's bottom line. Crucially, video games act as gateways into sports themselves.

For example, soccer's rising popularity in America is largely attributable to video games. Sixty-five percent of MLS fans were created because of EA Sports. In a 2019 interview, MLS Director James Ruth even stated, "Gaming is actually more important to [the MLS] than people playing soccer itself."[5] A further half of all US soccer fans claimed they were more interested in soccer because of its video game adaptation.[6] A similar story exists for the NBA in China, and for the NFL in Europe. Video games and the sports they represent are deeply synergistic.

So it was the NBA that moved first. On February 9, 2017, they announced the formation of an exclusive, digital esports league for the hit *NBA 2K* title.

The NBA 2K League broke new ground for three major reasons. First, the NBA 2K League represented a humongous investment in content. Sports gaming had flirted with esports for over a decade, with the FIFA eWorldcup tracing its roots as far back as 2004. But these early initiatives were characteristically tepid, little more than marketing expenditures to promote product. In contrast, the NBA 2K League was designed for media consumption. It featured all the hallmarks of a traditional basketball season: combine, draft, regular season, and championship play. It offered a slate of year-round activities fostering constant competition. And this steady content allowed the NBA 2K League to secure media deals, including broadcast rights and league-level sponsorships.[7,8]

Second, the NBA 2K League became the first traditional sports game to franchise. At inception, the league consisted of seventeen teams, each of which belonged to an existing NBA team. From the Milwaukee Bucks to the Boston Celtics, the majority of NBA brands created a digital roster (Bucks Gaming and Celtics Crossover Gaming, respectively). The presence of traditional sports teams brought a new level of legitimacy to esports. *NBA 2K* pros were promoted alongside mainline basketball stars and packaged with traditional sports sponsorships. As such, the NBA 2K League did more than bring the NBA into esports; it also dragged along its franchise owners with it.

But the NBA 2K League's final point of innovation is perhaps its most overlooked, but also its most critical: independence. The NBA 2K League was not established as a marketing arm of 2K Games, or an internal division of the NBA proper. It was founded as an independent joint venture between both. And this guaranteed a simple but groundbreaking truth: The NBA 2K League was created as an independent sport. It wasn't set up to sell more copies of the 2K game, or to help drive interest in mainline basketball (though both were secondary benefits). As an independent entity, the primary purpose of the NBA 2K League was to drive revenue and viewership of digital basketball.

The NBA created the 2K League as a joint venture to align incentives with its game developer. This separation also protected the NBA's brand: if the new league failed, the NBA could plausibly distance itself.

But independence also created a threat. Today, the NBA 2K League is functionally tied to the NBA, preventing direct competition. But as our society digitizes, as esports builds in popularity, might not conflicts emerge? What happens as augmented reality improves enough to mimic physical play? When athletes train in simulations instead of on the court? Or when consumers simply prefer virtual basketball, as it better reflects a digital-nativist lifestyle?

The NBA 2K League is a seismic shift in sports precisely because of what it might one day threaten: the collapse of sports proper. And this downfall may already be upon us. For example, the US Navy recently announced the cancellation of all its Super Bowl commercials in favor of esports advertising instead. It might seem crazy to think that a video game like NBA 2K could actually displace basketball itself. But remember: baseball would have seemed untouchable in the 1930s, too.

🏀

So how is the NBA 2K League doing?

Despite significant investment, viewership numbers for the league remain encouraging but relatively modest, peaking at around 40,000 fans per game.[9] And while major deals have been inked with AT&T, Intel, and State Farm, the future of the NBA 2K League remains undecided in the pantheon of esports.[10]

But why hasn't such a committed sports venture conquered esports? The answer comes down to the game itself.

The NBA 2K franchise is a phenomenal video game, beloved by millions of gamers worldwide. Each annual iteration boasts incredible graphics and visceral gameplay, always more compelling than the past year's edition. The game's quality explains its popularity, with every yearly release selling tens of millions of units.[11]

But this fantastic game isn't designed to be an esport. It's designed to be a *simulation*. Each NBA 2K game mimics basketball exactly. Every aspect of its design is focused on mirroring the physical sport: celebrity likenesses, realistic physics, interseasonal rule adjustments, and more. The NBA 2K game is built to be the closest thing to real basketball as can possibly be digitized.

The problem with a simulation is that it doesn't embrace its new medium. In most entertainment experiences, we accept that original works must be adapted to fit novel form factors. The Harry Potter movies are not line-by-line recreations of the Harry Potter books, despite the quality of the source material. A direct remake, failing to take advantage of the bigger spectacles possible within cinema and the faster pacing that moviegoers expect, would be boring.

The same holds true for NBA 2K. Even though the base material is incredible, it must also evolve. For the NBA 2K League to succeed, it must *stop mimicking* basketball.

NBA 2K's developers know change is required because some concessions have already been made. For example, NBA 2K matches don't run two hours, because the gaming medium demands faster competition. Instead, 2K games take about thirty-five minutes each. This adjustment may seem small, but many more like it already exist, and many more will follow.

And as the NBA 2K League evolves from basketball, the more it becomes a direct competitor. The less it promotes the traditional sport, the more it promotes itself. For this reason, above all else, the NBA 2K League may be on a one-way collision course with the NBA.

Today, traditional sports are, in some sense, the most exciting area of growth for esports. Because in the near future, the familiar will reinvent itself. Maybe it will begin with the NBA. Or maybe FIFA, the NFL, or MLB—all of which have announced recent plans to retrench in esports—will take the risk.[12]

But going forward, we will see new digital iterations of the traditional sports we love. And this change need not be entirely negative. Digital sports might also innovate the physical. Much as the instant replay forever changed how NFL teams are coached, could esports not eventually transform how physical games of basketball are played?

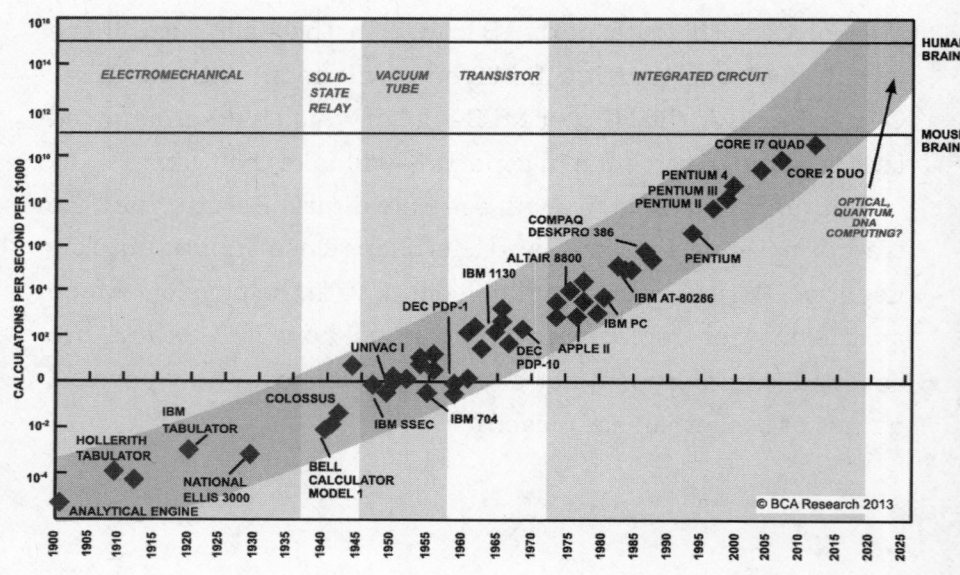

Moore's Law predicts an ever-accelerating pace of technological advancement.

EPILOGUE

EVENT HORIZON

If esports has come this far, this fast, where exactly is esports going? Now we will speculate aggressively (it's an epilogue, after all!). So suspend your disbelief for a moment, and glimpse beyond the event horizon of man and machine.

The future of esports is intimately tied to technological evolution. And the most well-established technological trend of our time is Moore's Law. Moore's Law states that computer processors get *faster* at an *exponential* rate. In practice this has most visibly played out in personal computing, with computational machines transformed from vacuum-sealed tubes, to desk-sized PCs, to globe-trotting laptops, and now to handheld smartphones.

Almost as a corollary, the computational growth predicted by Moore's Law also foretells digital miniaturization. As computers get faster, smaller computers can do bigger jobs. Miniaturization allows for technology to be meaningfully embedded into a wider range of objects and devices. And the natural culmination of this trend will likely be the integration of computers inside of humans.

If you don't believe embedded technology will revolutionize humanity, consider your cell phone. It's vital to your existence.

You carry it everywhere. It stores almost your entire life: your contacts, conversations, and even credit cards. Imagine the terror of losing your cell phone. There is arguably no purer definition of modern panic than an empty pocket after a subway ride. If your phone is so integral to your daily life, why wouldn't you want to guarantee it's always with you?

And this is how we begin to cross the digital divide.

"Injected technology won't start with actual injections," explains Dr. Jonghwan Lee, director of the Lab for Neuroengineering at Brown University. "It will begin unobtrusively. As *wearable* technology: clothing and jewelry."

That doesn't sound scary, does it? It would be useful. You would no longer need to remember your cell phone if your shirt subsumed its functionality. You may already have adopted wearable technology unknowingly, if you are one of the millions of consumers using a smart watch.

"Over time," continues Dr. Lee, "we will habituate to technology living against our bodies. Already, it doesn't feel strange that we carry around computers more powerful than *Apollo* 11 in our pockets. Technology will keep migrating closer, because it is convenient. The jump to true implantation will probably start with headphones. We already stick these wiry microchips inside our ears. And subdermal, tiny implantation near the ear and temple to record brainwaves makes functional sense. Plus, there is already cultural normalization. We already cut holes in our ears to embed metal and jewels. If we begin injecting computers into our ears, why not our fingertips? Why not our eyes? Eventually convenience and miniaturization will bury digitization deeper and deeper into the human body, until we reach that final frontier: the brain."

But the jump to brain implantation won't seem drastic. "It's likely surgery won't be required," Dr. Lee explains. "Elon Musk's

Neuralink is already working on tiny 'brain-reading' threads that can be implanted into the brain with relative unobtrusiveness. We might achieve mind-machine hybridization by injecting nano-machines that cross the blood-brain barrier, or a similar technology. Having a permanent computer in your head would likely only require a shot in the arm. That's just sci-fi acupuncture, right?"

Dr. Lee predicts this type of aggressive innovation happening *this* century. "My colleagues at Brown perform direct implantation today in their labs," explains Dr. Lee. "They literally build circuit boards into brains to help paralyzed people control external machines only by thinking. Also, many research labs across the globe are implanting circuit boards into eyes to help individuals with blindness see, like Geordi LaForge on *Star Trek: The Next Generation*. These technologies are not far from consumer applications. Plus, direct brain implantation is already standard procedure for certain illnesses, such as cochlear implants to restore hearing in people with deafness. I think mind-machine interfaces will become widespread by 2070, if not sooner."

Dr. Lee may be ambitious about the timeline, but his point is clear. Implantation is where humanity is going. Technology is moving into the body because we are inviting it. So if humanity trends toward transhumanism, what are the benefits of digital-physical integration?

At first, embedded technology will augment daily life. Think how convenient it would be, for example, to jot down the sudden idea you get during your morning shower, only by thinking. How about having Google Maps visible directly in your eye, without having to glance down at your phone every ten seconds? Imagine phone conversations on a crowded commute without needing to speak, or typing without needing to carry a bulky keyboard. And for the dystopian-minded among us, envision soldiers dominating the battlefields of the future with integrated satellite uplinks and positional visualizations.

Like all innovations, transhuman technology will begin with the functional, but it will quickly turn to entertainment. New classes of experience will emerge, built around hybridized digital-physical worlds. It won't be long before we're playing *World of Warcraft* in real life, with digital friends, battling monsters right in front of us that only we can see (the hit mobile game *Pokémon GO* already hints at this potential). After all, the universe is only as real as our brains perceive it to be, and implantation will allow us to directly control perception.

At first these entertainment fantasies will be experiences we just visit, but gradually they will linger. We will begin to socialize, to befriend, and to marry. We will conduct critical business and personal ceremonies, from mergers to weddings. After all, digital-hybridized experiences will look just like real life. They will feel just as real. And so we will spend more and more time inside them.

"Once the digital and physical aggressively intersect, we will eventually stop actively differentiating between what is real and what is illusory," Dr. Lee concludes. "Consider this: Today, fanatic gamers in Korea are already spending more than $100,000 in real money for single digital items—items that exist merely as a tiny bit of data in a game company's database. But though these items are illusory, the cognitive rewards they bestow—the joy of ownership, if you will—are nonetheless real. So what is the difference between owning a $100,000 digital sword and a $100,000 Ferrari, if both bring the same amount of happiness? Any distinction is a matter of form, not function. And distinctions of form are superficial at best. Think of files on your computer. You don't really care whether you open an image in a .jpeg or a .png format, because in the end, both formats display the same image. In the future, the digital and physical worlds will be just like two different file formats. We will interchange each seamlessly, and both will deliver happiness and meaning to the human experience."

In the future, we will—for better or for worse—enter the Matrix.

We may not *choose* to go all the way in, but we will at least spend a significant portion of our lives with the digital and physical intertwined. Technology will become synonymous with daily life.

So what does this all mean for esports?

First we must accept that at some point in the future, traditional sports will die for one practical reason: safety. In real sports, you can get hurt. But with computers that accurately simulate physical environments, and brains that are hooked directly into those worlds, we would not need to *play* real sports to *experience* real sports. These games would be strictly better if simulated.

And simulation would bring other advantages. Equality, for example. In a simulated environment, we could control for height, weight, limb length, natural hormone levels, and more. Essentially, we could make sports perfectly fair. Now anyone who loved a game could play it to the highest level their skill allowed, regardless of genetics.

Simulations would also permit longevity. In simulation, there is no degradation of the body, and age will cease to matter. The greatest titans of sporting history could endure for as a long as their minds allow—a thought likely to excite any fan who has had to watch their favorite quarterback retire.

But most of all, traditional sports will die because they will become boring, Instead, we will embrace the more fantastic conflicts permitted by digital-physical hybridization. We won't be shooting basketballs, but blasting targets in zero gravity with power weapons. We won't be kicking field goals, but propelling explosive bombs past mutant guardians. We won't be sliding into home plate, but teleporting into a dragon's lair to steal its gilded treasures. So if it isn't already obvious, these new experiences will be esports!

Today's competitive video games are the tip of this spear. They are the beginning of a trend that has nowhere near come to fruition. Just as it would have seemed crazy for the Wright brothers to prophesize landing on the moon, or for a pinball manufacturer to promise personalized computing, the future described sounds outlandish now.

But that does not make what's suggested here any less inevitable.

Esports are the future of all human competition. They are the first incarnation of a new medium of mind-versus-mind play. They are the beginning of freedom from the flesh, and the blossoming of the soul.

Esports is everything that is coming. Today they may live on a PC or a PlayStation, but they will quickly live everywhere and even inside us.

By embracing esports, we embrace the future. So go on Twitch and watch a streamer play *League of Legends*. Stop by your local esports stadium and catch a game of the Overwatch League. Download a game yourself (this author recommends *Hearthstone*) and start competing.

And if you're already a gamer, try engaging more broadly. Organize a local tournament or join a collegiate league.

Message your favorite pros on Twitter. Wear that fan jersey with pride. Do whatever it is you want to do. Just be a part of this movement. Because it's just beginning.

You just read *The Book of Esports*, but it was really a book about *us* all along. The future of humanity races ahead. And it's already a ton of fun.

APPENDIX

ESPORTS 101

If you've turned to this Appendix, chances are you are a neophyte when it comes to the world of modern gaming. There's nothing wrong with that. In fact, your interest in gaming should be applauded. Thank you for taking a chance on learning about the incredible world of esports, and how it is going to reshape all our lives.

We need to get you up to speed on modern gaming very quickly so you can appreciate the rest of this book, so we're going to run you through Esports 101 fast and in the most direct format possible: in a series of questions with short and simple answers. Each query is ordered in a logical progression, so in just a few pages you will go from esports basics to the big leagues.

What are esports?

Esports are competitive video games. Just like any competitive physical activity can be considered sport, any video game played competitively can be an esport.

How are esports different from regular video games?

Esports are video games *specifically designed* to reward skill and teamwork. They always involve some sort of head-to-head play against real human opponents. While regular video games may focus on storytelling, puzzles, or entertaining gameplay challenges, esports are specifically about competing directly with other people.

Why are esports hard to play?

Esports are difficult to play because they require multiple types of skill. A typical esports title requires *teamwork, strategy,* and *mechanical skills.*

Teamwork in esports is just the same as in traditional sports: you must coordinate actions with teammates in order to outplay opponents. Just as football and basketball have set plays, esports encourage orchestrated cooperation between players.

Strategy in esports is like military tactics: you must have a carefully considered plan to outwit your opponent, constantly updated based on events in-game. Just like chess masters adjust their strategies to evolving boards, esports players must continually reevaluate their plans to surprise and outwit the competition.

Mechanical skill in esports is akin to playing an instrument. Just as a pianist taps dozens of keys in a sequence to play a melody, esports athletes enter dozens of commands (typically via keyboard and mouse) to execute precision movements with precise timings.

What equipment is required to play esports?

Esports can technically be played on any digital device, from a cell phone to a home gaming console. However, because of the level of precision required to play esports well, most competitors use high-end gaming PCs paired with specially designed mechanical keyboards and mice. Just like soccer can technically be played in any shoe, but athletes gravitate to specially designed cleats, esports players prefer to use cutting-edge technology engineered for precision inputs.

How are esports competitions organized?

Esports competitions are organized almost exactly like traditional athletic competitions. Players form teams and enter tournaments, which are seeded using traditional brackets.

How do esports players make money?

Traditional athletes receive team salaries, prizing, and sponsorship deals. Esports athletes make money the same way. The industry is large enough that top players can earn over $20 million per year when combining all these revenue streams.

Where are esports tournaments broadcast?

Some esports tournaments are shown on terrestrial television, but most are broadcast online, via special websites like Twitch, which stream these tournaments in real time. Esports' younger audience (typically eighteen to thirty-five years old) prefers more digitally native content.

Who makes esports?

Esports are made by game developers, just like traditional video games. They are also published—or marketed and distributed—by traditional game publishers. In this regard, esports are no different from the original *Super Mario Bros.* However, the mechanisms of distribution have evolved from the days of Mario. Today, most esports titles aren't sold in stores but are downloadable for free online. The game publishers then make money by selling incremental upgrades to the basic experience.

Is esports like athletics, but for nerds?

Esports are like athletics in many ways: in particular, they require practice, skill, devotion, and teamwork. But just because esports are played on a computer doesn't mean they are for "nerds" (and, by the way, this author doesn't feel that being a "nerd" is a bad thing!). In fact, because of how competitive esports are, many people who enjoy traditional athletics supplement their competitive drive with esports. This is why so many NBA and NFL players love these games, too.

Should I be worried if my child is playing a lot of esports?

You should be worried if your child does too much of anything, from overeating to overexercising. There is nothing inherently wrong with esports. In fact, they teach many of the same skills and values as traditional athletics, which is part of the reason why many universities are embracing their adoption on campus. Playing esports with your child is also a great way to bond, just as playing traditional sports together is.

Are esports fun to watch?

Esports are just as fun to watch as traditional sports. If you've tuned into an esports broadcast and thought it was boring, it's likely because you didn't understand the game or its rules. Unlike traditional athletics, where it's relatively easy to appreciate the human skill required to tackle or kick, the fantastical, digital nature of esports can prove abstract and overwhelming for neophyte viewers. But with just a little game familiarity, esports become incredibly entertaining spectator experiences.

Are esports "pay-to-win"?

The term "pay-to-win" refers to using real money to purchase an unfair in-game advantage. Esports are not pay-to-win; if they were, they wouldn't require skill and so wouldn't be competitive. It is true that most modern esports encourage players to make in-game purchases; but these are typically cosmetic items that have no impact on actual gameplay.

ACKNOWLEDGMENTS

This book would not have been possible without the help of countless friends and colleagues, whose insights contributed substantially to this book and its development. In particular, I wish to thank Paul Dawalibi (who kindly also wrote the foreword to this book), Kevin Mitchell, Willy Lee, Joseph Ahn, Kurt Melcher, Matt Wyble, Nate Nanzer, Kevin Knocke, Frank Villarreal, Tim Loew, Alan Ritacco, Christian Volk, Josh Staley, Rohan Gopaldas, Ankith Harathi, Manoli Strecker, Peter Olson, and Hanna Halaburda.

Many pro gamers were also interviewed for this manuscript, and even if their comments didn't make the final book, their input remained invaluable to shaping my views on esports. I'd particularly like to thank Faraz Barmpar, William Barton, Allison Maino, Rosty Elkun, Faraaz Khan, and Vincent Chu.

I also want to extend my heartfelt thanks to my agent, Tim Wojcik of Levine Greenberg Rostan. And to my publisher, RosettaBooks and Arthur Klebanoff. Both believed in this work, and its potential, when there really wasn't much more to go on than an idea and a dream. I'd also like to express my deepest gratitude to my editor Francine LaSala, for her tireless and timely feedback. To Cassandra Hanjian, for her diligent work securing permissions. And to Max Saffer, for his extensive research identifying and vetting every source appearing in this book.

And finally, but perhaps most importantly, I want to thank my family. To my wife, Nahoko, who encouraged me to write this book in the first place (and who had most of its good ideas). To my mother, Jill Collis, for fostering my dreams of authorship for as long as I can remember. To my father, Professor David Collis, for listening patiently to my endless theories about the esports market. To my sisters, Charlotte and Emma, for their constant love and support. And most of all, to my two sons, George and Leo. I hope one day you will read this and be proud of your father's work.

I dedicate this book to all my family: past, present, and future.

ENDNOTES & SOURCES

PROLOGUE: PRESS START

1.   Market sizing in esports is notoriously challenging, since the result depends on your definition of esports. In this book, market size is based off proprietary research conducted by this author and Harvard PhD Joseph Ahn. Our analysis incorporates all direct esports revenues, including game sales, digital downloads, and streaming revenues attributable to esports, in addition to more traditional measures of esports like ticket sales and sponsorship revenues. For this reason, the esports market size in this book is larger than some other industry estimates. This author feels that including these additional revenue sources, and particularly publisher revenues, is required to accurately reflect the scale of the esports phenomenon.

2.   Nathan Meyer and Alan Wilson, "Video Game Industry Goes for the Win," Capital Group, accessed December 28, 2019, https://www.capitalgroup.com/europe/capitalideas/article/video-game-industry.html.

CHAPTER ONE: THE BITS AT THE BEGINNING

1.   While the invention of the pinball machine was much earlier in 1931, the original designs are a far cry from what we imagine today. The game looked much closer to skee ball and was arguably a game of luck.

2.   Pinball was first banned in New York in 1942 and remained so until 1976 because the mayor at the time believed it was a form of gambling that cheated kids out of their money. Many other states followed suit and some cities held this ban until as late as 2016.

3. Bertie the Brain's main purpose was to show off the additron tube, a type of electron tube that would hopefully make electronic computing more efficient. The machine didn't implement a real-time screen but instead utilized a less sophisticated lightbulb display, which some believe disqualifies this interactive experience from being classified as a video game.

CHAPTER TWO: SAVING THE PRINCESS

1. This book argues that the Intergalactic Olympics were the first-ever esports tournament. However, *Space Invaders* also occupies a notable place in gaming history, with its 1980 competitive event drawing over 10,000 participants and serving as a model for large-scale gaming activations going forward.

2. In 1979, Activision famously became the first third-party developer. It was comprised of former Atari employees who wanted better recognition, treatment, and compensation for their work. Third-party developers became a trend after their establishment, which flooded the market with games due to a lack of quality control.

3. Marc Cieslak, "Is the Japanese Gaming Industry in Crisis?" BBC Click, accessed January 10, 2020, http://news.bbc.co.uk/2/hi/programmes/click_online/9159905.stm.

CHAPTER THREE: GUILDS AND GLORY

1. Jay Serafino, "You've Got Mail: A History of AOL's Free Trial CDs," Mental Floss, accessed December 29, 2019, https://www.mentalfloss.com/article/87291/youve-got-mail-history-aols-free-trial-cds.

2. Mike Masnick, "The Economy of EverQuest Is About the Same as Bulgaria," TechDirt, accessed December 29, 2019, https://www.techdirt.com/articles/20020125/1249259.shtml.

3. Although this author firmly believes Horde is the correct choice. Lok'tar ogar!

4. This author is also aware that Iron Forge is a more appropriate location to list here, given that it is an Alliance stronghold. But we already have a Mage wielding Thunderfury; so don't be too judgmental. It's just an example!

5. Eliza Thompson, "3 Couples Talk About How World of Warcraft Brought Them Together," Cosmopolitan, accessed December 30, 2019, https://www.cosmopolitan.com/entertainment/movies/a59553/world-of-warcraft-wedding-stories/.

6. Lidia Warren, "Video Games Blamed for Divorce as Men 'Prefer World of Warcraft' to their Wives," Daily Mail, accessed January 10, 2020, https://www.dailymail.co.uk/news/article-1392561/World-Warcraft-video-games-blamed-divorce-men-prefer-wives.html.

CHAPTER FOUR: THE REVOLUTION IS TELEVISED

1. Dean Takahashi, "Google's $1B Purchase of Twitch Confirmed (updated)," Venture Beat, accessed December 30, 2019, https://venturebeat.com/2014/07/24/googles-1b-purchase-of-twitch-confirmed-joins-youtube-for-new-video-empire/.

2. "Twitch Statistics and Charts," TwitchTracker, accessed December 30, 2019, https://twitchtracker.com/statistics.

3. "World Cyber Games USA 2005," Esportspedia, accessed December 30, 2019, https://www.esportspedia.com/halo/World_Cyber_Games_USA_2005.

4. Adam Newell, "What Does Kappa Mean?" Dot Esports, accessed December 30, 2019, https://dotsports.com/culture/news/kappa-meaning-twitch-meme-15708.

5. Paul Tassi, "Ninja's New 'Fortnite' Twitch Records 5 Million Followers, 250,000 Subs, $875,000+ a Month," Forbes, accessed January 10, 2020, https://www.forbes.com/sites/insertcoin/2018/04/07/ninjas-new-fortnite-twitch-records-5-million-followers-250000-subs-875000-a-month/.

CHAPTER FIVE: CRAFTING WITH THE STARS

1. Richard Moss, "Build, Gather, Brawl, Repeat: The History of Real-Time Strategy Games," Ars Technica, accessed December 30, 2019, https://arstechnica.com/gaming/2017/09/build-gather-brawl-repeat-the-history-of-real-time-strategy-games/.

2. Lest this author appear unaware: The 1984 movie Dune was itself based on the incredible books by Frank Herbert. He is the Kwisatz Haderach!

3. Sarah Jacobsson Purewal, "StarCraft II Breaks Game Sales Records,"

PCWorld, accessed January 10, 2020, https://www.pcworld.com/
article/202534/starcraft_ii_breaks_game_sales_records.html.

4. "South Korea: The Most Wired Place on Earth," PBS Frontline World,
accessed December 30, 2019, http://www.pbs.org/frontlineworld/stories/
south_korea802/video/video_index.html.

5. "Hours Worked," OECD Data, accessed December 30, 2019, https://data.
oecd.org/emp/hours-worked.htm.

6. "BoxeR," Liquipedia, accessed December 30, 2019, https://liquipedia.net/
StarCraft2/BoxeR.

7. "Lim 'BoxeR' Yo Hwan — StarCraft II Player," Esports Earnings, accessed
December 30, 2019, https://www.esportsearnings.com/players/1047-boxer-
lim-yo-hwan.

8. Christina H., "5 Insane True Facts About StarCraft: The Professional
Sport," Cracked, accessed December 30, 2019, https://www.cracked.com/
article_18763_5-insane-true-facts-about-StarCraft-professional-sport.
html.

CHAPTER SIX: RIOT IN THE STREETS

1. B. Wiley, "Warcraft III Shatters Sales Records," IGN, accessed December
30, 2019, https://www.ign.com/articles/2002/07/22/warcraft-iii-shatters-
sales-records.

2. The merger actually occurred between Vivendi Games, Blizzard's parent
company, and Activision. But we simplify the narrative here to avoid
distraction.

3. Eddie Makuch, "Riot: League of Legends Has 12 Million Daily 'Active'
Players," Game Spot, accessed December 30, 2019, https://www.gamespot.
com/articles/riot-league-of-legends-has-12-million-daily-active-
players/1100-6398154/.

4. Mike Stubbs, "The International 9 'Dota 2' Tournament Prize Pool
Breaks $30 Million," Forbes, accessed December 30, 2019, https://www.
forbes.com/sites/mikestubbs/2019/07/27/the-international-9-dota-2-
tournament-prize-pool-breaks-30-million/#76a54c4b2c07.

5. Jeff Grubb, "Dota 2 Makes $18M per Month for Valve—but League of Legends Makes That Much Every 5 Days," Venture Beat, accessed December 30, 2019, https://venturebeat.com/2015/03/24/dota-2-makes-18m-per-month-for-valve-but-league-of-legends-makes-that-much-every-5-days/.

6. "Blizzard, Valve Settle DOTA Lawsuit," Cinema Blend, accessed December 30, 2019, https://www.cinemablend.com/games/Blizzard-Valve-Settle-DOTA-Lawsuit-42430.html.

7. Mike Schramm, "Blizzard and Valve Settle DOTA Argument, Blizzard DOTA Is Now Blizzard All-Stars," Engadget, accessed December 30, 2019, https://www.engadget.com/2012-05-11-blizzard-and-valve-settle-dota-argument-blizzard-dota-is-now-bl.html.

8. This was a moment of heartbreak for this author, who greatly enjoyed his time tanking as Muradin in the Nexus.

CHAPTER SEVEN: WATCHING OVER US

1. Andy Chalk, "Titan Cancellation May Have Cost Blizzard More Than $50 Million," PC Gamer, accessed January 10, 2020, https://www.pcgamer.com/titan-cancellation-may-have-cost-blizzard-more-than-50-million/.

2. Allegra Frank, "Overwatch Open Beta Attracts Nearly 10M Players," Polygon, accessed January 10, 2020, https://www.polygon.com/2016/5/13/11672382/overwatch-open-beta-record-blizzard-entertainment.

3. Brian Crecente, "'Overwatch' Tops 40 Million Players as Game Hits Two-Year Anniversary," Variety, accessed January 10, 2020, https://variety.com/2018/gaming/news/overwatch-two-year-anniversary-1202820958/.

4. Paresh Dave, "The NFL of E-Sports? Blizzard Wants to Create 'Overwatch' League with City-Specific Video Game Fans," Los Angeles Times, accessed December 30, 2019, https://www.latimes.com/business/technology/la-fi-tn-overwatch-esports-blizzcon-20161103-story.html.

5. Ben Fischer, "Activision Blizzard Sells Seven Teams for Startup Overwatch League," SBJ Daily, accessed December 30, 2019, https://www.sportsbusinessdaily.com/Daily/Issues/2017/07/12/Leagues-and-Governing-Bodies/Overwatch-League.aspx.

6. Imad Khan, "Riot Releases Details on NA LCS Franchising with $10M Flat-Fee Buy-In," ESPN, accessed December 30, 2019, https://www.espn.com/esports/story/_/id/19511222/riot-releases-details-na-lcs-franchising-10m-flat-fee-buy-in.

7. Alex Stedman, "Overwatch League's Grand Finals Grows 16% in Average Viewers from Last Year," Variety, accessed December 30, 2019, https://variety.com/2019/digital/news/overwatch-league-grand-finals-viewership-2019-1203357584/.

CHAPTER EIGHT: LOOKING FOR GROUP

1. "Overall Esports Stats for 1999," Esports Earnings, accessed December 31, 2019, https://www.esportsearnings.com/history/1999/teams.

2. Duncan "Thorin" Shields, "The History and Formation of Cloud 9 — Part 1 of the Cloud 9 Story," onGamers News, accessed December 31, 2019, https://web.archive.org/web/20150216054323/http://www.ongamers.com/articles/the-history-and-formation-of-cloud-9-part-1-of-the-cloud-9-story/1100-1302/.

3. Mike Ozanian and Christina Settimi, "The World's Most Valuable Esports Companies," Forbes, accessed December 31, 2019, https://www.forbes.com/sites/mikeozanian/2018/10/23/the-worlds-most-valuable-esports-companies-1/#2d3d8a186a6e.

4. Pete Volk, "Rick Fox Purchases League of Legends Team for Reported $1 Million, Will Rebrand as Echo Fox," SBNation, accessed December 31, 2019, https://www.sbnation.com/2015/12/18/10602006/echo-fox-league-of-legends-rick-fox-gravity.

5. Noah Smith, "'It's Not as Awesome as People Imagine': Esports Players Say 'Dream Job' Is More than Fun and Games," The Washington Post, accessed December 31, 2019, https://www.washingtonpost.com/sports/2018/12/13/its-not-awesome-people-imagine-esports-players-say-dream-job-is-more-than-fun-games/.

6. "New York Yankees 2020 Payroll," Spotrac, accessed December 31, 2019, https://www.spotrac.com/mlb/new-york-yankees/payroll/.

7. Yusuf Khan, "'It's About Controlling Your Dollar': The Inside Story of How the New York Yankees and the Dallas Cowboys Became the Most Valuable Franchises in Sports," Markets Insider, accessed December 31, 2019, https://markets.businessinsider.com/news/stocks/how-dallas-cowboys-and-new-york-yankees-most-valuable-franchises-2019-7-1028414397.

CHAPTER TEN: KETCHUP OR MUSTARD?

1. Kirsten Acuna, "Here's Why 'The Hunger Games' Is Not 'Battle Royale,'" Business Insider, accessed December 31, 2019, https://www.businessinsider.com/the-hunger-games-is-not-battle-royale-despite-many-similarities-2012-4.

2. Brendan Sinclair, "PlayerUnknown's Battlegrounds Does $11 Million in Three Days," GamesIndustry.biz, accessed December 31, 2019, https://www.gamesindustry.biz/articles/2017-03-27-playerunknowns-battlegrounds-does-usd11-million-in-three-days.

3. Sean Hollister, "PUBG Sells 6 Million Copies—and Seems to be Accelerating," CNET, accessed December 31, 2019, https://www.cnet.com/news/pubg-playerunknowns-battlegrounds-6-million-tournament-prizes/.

4. Andrew Webster, "As PUBG Hits Version 1.0, It Now Has 30 Million Players," The Verge, accessed December 31, 2019, https://www.theverge.com/2017/12/21/16806758/playerunknowns-battlegrounds-pubg-30-million-sales.

5. Michael McWhertor, "PUBG Reaches 50M Copies Sold, 400M Total Players," Polygon, accessed December 31, 2019, https://www.polygon.com/2018/6/19/17478476/playerunknowns-battlegrounds-sales-pubg-number-of-players.

6. "Fortnite Battle Royale Goes Free for Everyone on Sept. 26," Epic Games, accessed December 31, 2019, https://www.epicgames.com/fortnite/en-US/news/fortnite-battle-royale-goes-free.

7. Haydn Taylor, "Fortnite Reaches Ten Million Players," GamesIndustry.biz, accessed December 31, 2019, https://www.gamesindustry.biz/articles/2017-10-11-fortnite-reaches-ten-million-players.

8. Andrew Webster, "Fortnite Made an Estimated $2.4 Billion Last Year," The Verge, accessed December 31, 2019, https://www.theverge.com/2019/1/16/18184302/fortnite-revenue-battle-pass-earnings-2018.

9. Cecilia D'Anastasio, "Report: Fortnite Developers Describe Severe Ongoing Crunch," Kotaku, accessed December 31, 2019, https://kotaku.com/report-fortnite-developers-are-severely-overworked-1834243520.

10. This chapter has focused on the success of *PUBG* as an esport. But taking a broader view, *PUBG* did not fail entirely. In fact, its mobile version has proved incredibly successful. Thanks to a Tencent-backed relaunch as Game for Peace in China, *PUBG* Mobile has continued to break sales records in Asia. But don't be fooled. *PUBG* had a bigger opportunity: to define the next generation of global esports. And it was *Fortnite*, not *PUBG*, that undeniably claimed this crown.

11. Dave Thier, "'Apex Legends' Made More Money in Its First Month Than Any Other Free-to-Play Game, Ever," Forbes, accessed December 31, 2019, https://www.forbes.com/sites/davidthier/2019/03/22/apex-legends-made-more-money-in-its-first-month-than-any-other-free-to-play-game-ever/#373426dd7e18.

12. Bijan Stephan, "Fortnite's Overall Revenue Slipped in 2019, but It Was Still the Biggest Earner of the Year," The Verge, accessed January 10, 2020, https://www.theverge.com/2020/1/2/21046920/fortnite-revenue-drop-superdata-nielsen-2019-earnings.

CHAPTER ELEVEN: VISUALIZING WAR

1. Joseph Ahn and William Collis, "Play to Win: A Deep Dive Into Esports Value Chains," white paper pending publication.

2. Hilary Russ, "Global Esports Revenue to Top $1 Billion in 2019: Report," *Reuters*, accessed April 27, 2020, https://www.reuters.com/article/us-videogames-outlook/global-esports-revenues-to-top-1-billion-in-2019-report-idUSKCN1Q11XY.

3. Statista Research Department, "Sports Sponsorship – Statistics &Facts," Statista, accessed December 31, 2019, https://www.statista.com/topics/1382/sports-sponsorship/.

4. Steven Messner, "Every Game Company That Tencent Has Invested In," PC Gamer, accessed December 31, 2019, https://www.pcgamer.com/everygame-company-that-tencent-has-invested-in/.

5. Jared Canfield, "12 Movies So Expensive They Bankrupted Their Studio," Screen Rant, accessed December 31, 2019, https://screenrant.com/movies-bankrupted-studios/.

6. *Reuters*, "Dignitas Return to LCS with Acquisition of Clutch Gaming," ESPN, accessed December 31, 2019, https://www.espn.com/esports/story/_/id/26914313/dignitas-return-lcs-acquisition-clutch-gaming.

7. Austen Goslin, "Immortals Gaming Acquires Infinite Esports Parent-Company of OpTic Gaming and Houston Outlaws," Polygon, accessed December 31, 2019, https://www.polygon.com/2019/6/12/18663066/immortals-gaming-buys-infinite-esports-optic-gaming-houston-outlawsla-valiant-overwatch-league.

8. Dean Takahashi, "Immortals Raises $30 Million for Esports Expansion, Acquires Brazil's Gamers Club," Venture Beat, accessed December 31, 2019, https://venturebeat.com/2019/05/01/immortals-raises-30-million-foresports-expansion-acquires-brazils-gamers-club/.

9. Nick Geracie, "NYXL Owner Andbox Unveils New Gaming x Streetwear Collection," Inven Global, accessed February 12, 2020, https://www.invenglobal.com/articles/8725/nyxl-owner-andbox-unveils-new-gaming-xstreetwear-collection.

10. Steve Dent, "Echo Fox Loses its Pro 'League of Legends' Franchise Spot," Engadget, accessed December 31, 2019, https://www.engadget.com/2019/08/15/echo-fox-cut-from-lcl/.

11. Nicole Carpenter, "Overwatch Stats Program Visor CEO Responds to Blizzard's Ban," DOT Esports, accessed December 31, 2019, https://dotesports.com/overwatch/news/overwatch-stats-program-visor-ceoresponds-to-blizzards-ban.

12. Christopher Dring, "What's Next for Activision Blizzard's $300m Merchandise Business," Game Industry, accessed December 31, 2019, https://www.gamesindustry.biz/articles/2017-10-20-whats-next-foractivision-blizzards-usd300m-merchandise-business.

13. Richard Lewis, "Leaked Call of Duty Franchise League Deck Reveals Minimum Salaries, Team Sizes, Expansion Plans," Dexerto, accessed December 31, 2019, https://www.dexerto.com/call-of-duty/leaked-deckreveals-new-details-of-upcoming-call-of-duty-franchise-league-926192.

14. Richard Lewis, "Leaked Overwatch League Memo Drastically Shifts Housing Requirements, Confirms 'Luxury Tax,'" Dexerto, accessed December 31, 2019, https://www.dexerto.com/overwatch/overwatch-leagueleak-housing-requirements-luxury-tax-888650.

15. Andrew Hayward, "Rainbow Six Siege to Expand Revenue-Sharing Pilot Program," The Esports Observer, accessed December 31, 2019, https://esportsobserver.com/rainbow-six-pro-league-rev-sharing/.

16. "The Business of Baseball," Forbes, accessed January 10, 2020, https://www.forbes.com/mlb-valuations/list/#tab:overall.

17. Tom Bogert, "Atlanta United Retain Top Spot in Forbes' Annual MLS Team Valuations," MLS Soccer, accessed January 10, 2020, https://www.mlssoccer.com/post/2019/11/04/atlanta-united-retain-top-spot-forbesannual-mls-team-valuations.

CHAPTER TWELVE: FLAWLESS VICTORY

1. Darren Geeter, "Your Kid's Fortnite Obsession Could Land Them a College Scholarship," CNBC, accessed January 10, 2020, https://www.cnbc.com/2018/08/16/fortnite-coaches-parents-kids-college-scholarships.html.

2. Richard Cobbett, "The Legacy of Quake, 20 Years Later," PC Gamer, accessed December 31, 2019, https://www.pcgamer.com/the-legacy-of-quake-20-years-later/.

3. Daniel Wolfe, "Broadcasting Video Games Is Raising Millions for Charities," Quartz, accessed December 31, 2019, https://qz.com/1712428/how-games-done-quick-raises-millions-with-twitch-charity-streams/.

4. Judy Heflin, "ESL Brings Esports to Disney Programming with ESL Brawlers and ESL Speedrunners," ESL Magazine, accessed December 31, 2019, https://www.eslgaming.com/article/esl-brings-esports-disney-programming-esl-brawlers-and-esl-speedrunners-3624.

5. "Super Mario Bros.," Speedrun.com, accessed December 31, 2019, https://www.speedrun.com/smb1.

6. Graham Ashton, "Esports Arena to Host $5,000 Speedrunning PvP 'Grudge Match,'" The Esports Observer, accessed December 31, 2019, https://esportsobserver.com/esports-arena-speedrunning/.

7. "Welcome CLG Speedrunning," CLG, accessed December 31, 2019, https://www.clg.gg/news/2018/10/02/clg-speedrunners.

CHAPTER THIRTEEN: THE NEW KID AT SCHOOL

1. Dean Takahashi, "PlayVS Raises $50 Million More for High School Esports Platform," VentureBeat, accessed January 10, 2020, https://venturebeat.com/2019/09/18/playvs-raises-50-million-more-for-high-school-esports-platform/.

2. Kevin J. Ryan, "In Just One Year, This Startup Got Two-Thirds of U.S. High Schools to Adopt E-Sports," Inc., accessed January 10, 2020, https://www.inc.com/kevin-j-ryan/playvs-esports-high-schools-series-c-delane-parnell.html.

3. Andrew Hayward, "NCAA Votes to Not Govern Collegiate Esports," The Esports Observer, accessed January 10, 2020, https://esportsobserver.com/ncaa-nogo-collegiate-esports/.

4. Tom Schad, "NCAA Tables Possibility of Overseeing Esports," USA Today, accessed January 10, 2020, https://www.usatoday.com/story/sports/college/2019/05/21/ncaa-and-esports-not-just-yet-organization-tables-possibility/3751122002/.

CHAPTER FOURTEEN: A LEAGUE OF THEIR OWN

1. "Sports," Gallup, accessed December 31, 2019, https://news.gallup.com/poll/4735/sports.aspx.

2. "History of Instant Replay," NFL Football Operations, accessed January 1, 2020, https://operations.nfl.com/the-game/history-of-instant-replay/.

3. Annie Pei, "This Esports Giant Draws in More Viewers than the Super Bowl, and It's Expected to Get Bigger," CNBC, accessed January 10, 2020, https://www.cnbc.com/2019/04/14/league-of-legends-gets-more-viewers-than-super-bowlwhats-coming-next.html.

4. Jason Wilson, "FIFA 19 and FIFA 18 Had 45 Million Unique Console and PC Players in EA's Fiscal 2019," VentureBeat, accessed January 10, 2020, https://venturebeat.com/2019/05/07/fifa-19-and-fifa-18-had-45-million-unique-console-and-pc-players-in-eas-fiscal-2019/.

5.   Bob Garcia, "FIFA Video Game Is Bringing More Fans to Soccer Than Does Real Soccer," The Big Blind, accessed January 1, 2020, https://www.americascardroom.eu/poker-blog/2019/06/fifa-video-game-is-bringing-more-fans-to-soccer-than-does-real-soccer/.

6.   Rich Luker, "How Video Game Technology Creates Sports Fans," Sports Business Journal, accessed January 10, 2020, https://www.sportsbusinessdaily.com/Journal/Issues/2015/01/26/Research-and-Ratings/UpNext-with-Rich-Luker.aspx?hl=video%20games.

7.   Brendan Sinclair, "Twitch Signs Multi-Year Deal with NBA 2K League," Gamesindustry.biz, accessed January 1, 2020, https://www.gamesindustry.biz/articles/2018-04-18-twitch-signs-multi-year-deal-with-nba-2k-league.

8.   Sam Minton, "NBA 2K League Gains Major Sponsorship for Next Season," Apptrigger, accessed January 1, 2020, https://apptrigger.com/2019/02/07/nba-2k-league-gains-major-sponsorship-next-season/.

9.   "NBA 2K League 2019," Esports Charts, accessed January 1, 2020, https://escharts.com/tournaments/nba-2k/nba-2k-league-2019-regular-season.

10. Adam Fitch, "NBA 2K League Receives Sponsorship from AT&T," Esports Insider, accessed January 1, 2020, https://esportsinsider.com/2019/02/nba-2k-league-att-sponsorship/.

11. Mike Minotti, "NBA 2K Series Closes in on 90 Million Sold," VentureBeat, accessed January 1, 2020, https://venturebeat.com/2019/02/06/nba-2k-series-closes-in-on-90-million-sold/.

12. Tom Bassam, "'Esports Is a Weak Area for MLB', Admits Commissioner," SportsPro, accessed January 1, 2020, http://www.sportspromedia.com/news/mlb-esports-rob-manfred-commissioner.

IMAGE CREDITS

ABOUT THE AUTHOR

WILLIAM "THE PROFESSOR" COLLIS graduated from Amherst College cum laude and Harvard Business School as a Baker Scholar. After working for BCG and Hasbro, William co-founded and sold the esports coaching platform Gamer Sensei, raising over $6 million in venture capital. William is currently co-owner and co-founder of the pro esports organization Team Genji, ranked as the #1 *Hearthstone* team in the world. William is the subject of the Harvard Business School case "Choosing the Right Esports Business Model," and co-author of the award-winning Harvard Business School case "One Game to Rule Them All." He is also a frequent esports contributor to numerous publications, including the *Japan Times*, with his most popular article, "Super Mario Syndrome" receiving wide reprints in Asia. William earned his nickname, "The Professor" as co-founder and co-host of the popular *Business of Esports* podcast, where you can listen to his views on the gaming industry, its growth, and its future every week.